CAST

(In Order of Appearance)

Edward Barbee

Helen Foster

Tom

Douglas MacKelwaine

Woodrow W. O'Malley

Waiter

Butch Flowers

Joey Hallop

Gladys Bagley

Alexander Brown

Turner

Officer John

Police Sergeant

Harold Haskell

Lieutenant Muller

SYNOPSIS OF SCENES

Act One

Scene 1: The outer office of Edward Barbee, attorney-at-law. Six P.M.

Scene 2: The elevator of the building.

Scene 3: A small restaurant.

Scene 4: Room 1640 of the Mansvoort Hotel. Eight P.M.

Scene 5: Barbee's outer office. Next morning.

Act Two

Scene 1: Room 1640 of the Mansvoort Hotel. Three weeks later.

Scene 2: The small restaurant.

Scene 3: The 47th Street Police Station. Nine P.M.

Scene 4: Room 1640.

WATCH THE BIRDIE

ACT I

SCENE 1

SCENE: *The outer office of Edward Barbee, attorney-at-law. Six P.M. A small, well-worn office, including a leather couch. Entrance to Barbee's office is Upper Right, Outer Door, Rear Left.*

A telephone is ringing as the Curtain rises. It rings. From Barbee's office comes Barbee, casually, smoking a pipe. He leans against the door jamb, looking at the ringing phone. Barbee is pleasant, hard working, fifty, likable. Now the second phone begins to ring, distinct from the first. Barbee looks from one to the other.

Through the Outer Door comes Helen, the heroine of our story. She is twenty-two, beautiful, desirable, efficient, practical, and quite possibly a virgin. She is carrying a hand towel and the cosmetic accoutrements for face changing at the end of the day.

BARBEE. (*As she enters.*) The phone's ringing. (*As she crosses to them.*) I'm avoiding Paley! I'm not in! (*Helen quickly picks up the first one. She has a charming voice, too.*)
HELEN. (*Into phone.*) One moment, please. (*She puts it down as she picks up the other.*) Edward Barbee, attorney-at-law . . . Hello, Mister Benson . . . I sent the transcript this morning . . . two copies . . . You're quite welcome . . . (*She hangs up and takes the other phone.*) Edward Barbee, attorney-at-law . . . (*For Barbee's benefit.*) Yes, Mister Wilkins . . . They've been subpoenaed . . . Judge Hofsteder's court . . . (*Smile for the compliment.*) Thank *you.* (*She hangs up and sits, stowing away her paraphernalia.*)
BARBEE. Don't let Paley get to me. He wants a postponement on the Hooper case.

HELEN. Can't he get it by himself?
BARBEE. He can, but he's not as smart as you. (*The phone rings again.*)
HELEN. Edward Barbee, attorney-at-law . . . One moment, please. (*Hand over the phone.*) Mister Richards . . . (*Barbee goes to the phone. He sits on the desk.*)
BARBEE. What's up? . . . (*Not pleased.*) That's pretty careless! . . . It's after six o'clock, my girl's going home! . . . I'll ask her . . . (*To Helen.*) What are you doing tonight?
HELEN. Washing my hair.
BARBEE. I'll pay for your dinner and a hair wash. Need something notarized at eight o'clock tonight.
HELEN. (*Thinks.*) Okay.
BARBEE. (*Into phone.*) You're in luck. See you there. 'Bye. (*He hangs up.*) Show up at the Mansvoort Hotel. Room sixteen forty.
HELEN. (*Noting on a pad.*) Mansvoort, sixteen forty, eight o'clock. (*She will take her notary seal and put it in her purse.*)
BARBEE. How much longer you staying on this job?
HELEN. (*She looks sharply to him.*) Why?
BARBEE. (*Slumping into the couch.*) Secretaries usually last about two years and get married. You've used up the two years.
HELEN. Is this a roundabout way to tell me you'd like me to leave?
BARBEE. Good grief, no! You can stay forever. Breaking in a new secretary is worse than breaking in a new wife. You have to be polite, you have to watch your language, you have to be careful they don't think you're making a pass at them, I tell you it's a hell of a strain.
HELEN. (*Mock.*) Why, Mister Barbee, you never made a pass at me.
BARBEE. I never made a pass at any of 'em! The one ahead of you quit because she said I was always looking at her bosom! I wasn't looking at her bosom, when I dictate I'm concentrating, her bosom just happened to be where I was looking!
HELEN. Next time get a girl with a higher bosom.
BARBEE. (*He thinks about it.*) Little difficult explaining that to the agency. You got any husband candidates picked out?
HELEN. Oh, there's a couple of fellows I think I can get to their knees.
BARBEE. You only need one, you know.

HELEN. Maybe if I only had one it'd be easier to make my mind up.
BARBEE. You must like one better than the other?
HELEN. No. Like 'em both. Even Steven.
BARBEE. Then you don't like either enough.
HELEN. I've thought of that.
BARBEE. Keep looking.
HELEN. I'll do that.
BARBEE. Don't go cheap. You're a beautiful, desirable, intelligent girl and you can get any man you put your mind to.
HELEN. Why, thank you, Mister Barbee. A girl can use that at the end of a hard day.
BARBEE. I hope sitting in this office hasn't given you a cockeyed view of marriage. Once in a while a marriage doesn't end in a divorce court.
HELEN. Oh, I'm not against marriage. Looking forward to it, as a matter of fact. For one thing it'll get me out of the subway. I think more girls get married to get out of the subway than any other reason. I'm in favor of marriage. It just seems to come too soon. For a girl, anyway.
BARBEE. How's that?
HELEN. Well, you finally grow up and get away from mamma and step into a big, exciting world, and before you really get started to enjoy it some man comes along and puts you in a three room apartment with a play pen in the living room. And there you stay.
BARBEE. In a good marriage a wife isn't excluded from her husband's world. She's a partner. (*Solemnly.*) I don't think I could put up with most of this nonsense if I didn't have my wife to share it.
HELEN. (*Touched.*) You're an unusual husband and your wife's very lucky, Mister Barbee.
BARBEE. (*Smiles.*) Thank you. A man can use that at the end of a hard day.
HELEN. She's also lucky her husband's a lawyer, so there's something to talk about. I'm in the market for a conductor on a Fifth Avenue bus! At least he travels and meets interesting people! (*Tom enters. Tom is the building handyman, the assistant to the superintendent. He wears the uniform of his calling, and a cap,*

which he takes off. He is sixty, gentle, and on intimate terms with all the tenants.)

BARBEE. Hi, Tom.

TOM. Hello, Mister Barbee. Hello, Miss Foster.

HELEN. Hello, Tom.

TOM. Miss Foster, do you recall a young man who gets off the elevator at the ninth floor? He was in the elevator when you came back from lunch today.

HELEN. Dark hair, blue suit, straight nose, fair complexion, button down shirt and bow tie. (*Going straight on, but smiling.*) No, I didn't notice him.

BARBEE. (*He stares at her, impressed.*) For Pete's sake!

HELEN. (*Grinning.*) And he's not even my type.

TOM. (*Seriously.*) The young man'd like to meet you.

BARBEE. Well, now!

TOM. He says he's waited in the lobby for the last three weeks until you came back from lunch so he could ride up in the elevator with you.

HELEN. He missed a couple of days.

BARBEE. I think that's very touching. What does this young man do?

HELEN. If he drives a Fifth Avenue bus I'm his.

TOM. (*Straight.*) Oh no, he doesn't drive a bus! He's doing some work in this building for Peabody and Company. He's an accountant.

HELEN. No, Tom. I'm not interested in a man who sends someone else to speak for him. Tell him to go away.

TOM. He didn't send me. He gave me five dollars to stop the elevator when you go home tonight.

BARBEE. What's that?

TOM. I won't do it if you're against it. I thought if you didn't mind talking to him I'd make the five dollars. He says he wants to ask you to dinner, but I keep the five dollars whether you go to dinner or not.

BARBEE. How does he expect you to stop the elevator?

TOM. I wait in the hall until Miss Foster goes in and I stop it from the switch box.

BARBEE. And then what's supposed to happen?

TOM. Well, when it stops he'll call me on the elevator-telephone, and I'll say for nobody to worry, it'll be fixed in a couple of

minutes. That's all he wants for the five dollars, a couple of minutes.
BARBEE. Jack the Ripper only needed thirty seconds. Give him back the five dollars.
TOM. If you say so, Mister Barbee. That's why I asked.
HELEN. Oh, pull the switch, Tom.
BARBEE. You mean you're going to talk to him?
HELEN. No, but I'll listen. For two minutes I can give him a fish-eye and Tom'll keep the five dollars. Just two minutes, Tom!
TOM. Yes ma'am.
BARBEE. (*Admiringly.*) Women are trickier than men. I always thought so.
HELEN. We have to be. Look what we're up against. Elevator stoppers! (*And Douglas MacKelwaine enters. He is forty, in a pin stripe suit, rather a clothes horse, a large likable, rich man. He carries a small paper wrapped parcel. He looks at Tom, a stranger to him.*)
BARBEE. (*Not rising from the couch.*) Join us!
TOM. I'll be in the hall, Miss Foster. (*MacKelwaine watches him go.*)
MACKELWAINE. Good evening, Miss Foster.
HELEN. Good evening, Mister MacKelwaine.
MACKELWAINE. (*To Barbee.*) I want a drink!
BARBEE. (*To Helen.*) Bartender!
HELEN. (*Getting up, and starting toward the office, remembering.*) You're—Canadian Club and soda?
MACKELWAINE. Very little soda today. (*She goes. He sits next to Barbee on the couch, heavily.*) You know, I don't like being divorced for adultery. Getting caught in a hotel room with a strange woman and having my picture taken is embarrassing.
BARBEE. Well, there are other grounds.
MACKELWAINE. Let's hear them.
BARBEE. There's cruel and inhuman treatment. Would you be willing to say in court you've struck your wife?
MACKELWAINE. I'd be proud to. I didn't have the guts.
BARBEE. You can have a very simple divorce if you've been in jail for three consecutive years.
MACKELWAINE. It's almost worth it.
BARBEE. Or if she's abandoned you for two years.
MACKELWAINE. No such luck.

BARBEE. How about a separation decree and living apart for two years?
MACKELWAINE. Don't want to wait that long.
BARBEE. The Legislature leaves you only two more—sodomy and homosexuality. Take your pick.
MACKELWAINE. Adultery's fine.
BARBEE. I thought so.
MACKELWAINE. What about the property settlement? Did my dear, damn wife agree to the changes?
BARBEE. She agreed.
MACKELWAINE. She's pretty tricky. Did she sign it?
BARBEE. She did. They're bringing the document to the hotel. Then you'll sign it and Miss Foster'll notarize it, all before you put one pink toe into bed.
MACKELWAINE. I'll say. (*He thinks.*) Who am I getting in bed with?
BARBEE. (*Enjoying the ritual talk.*) The co-respondent in the case, with whom your wife has reason to believe you have had dalliance on diverse occasions, to which defendant does not reply.
MACKELWAINE. Yeah, but who is she?
BARBEE. She's a professional co-respondent. Very reliable, you're in good hands.
MACKELWAINE. What do you mean "good hands"?
BARBEE. She knows her job.
MACKELWAINE. Will you cut out all the pussyfooting. Yes or no, am I supposed to do anything or not?
BARBEE. Not only are you not supposed to do anything but should you get it in your head to try Miss Bagley will throw you out the window!
MACKELWAINE. Really? I'm relieved to hear it.
BARBEE. (*Looks at him keenly.*) You don't look relieved.
MACKELWAINE. Oh I don't claim I'm above— (*He searches for the word.*) —dalliance—don't get me wrong—but I don't like to be pushed.
BARBEE. Well, calm yourself, Miss Bagley won't push you. This is just business to her. All you're expected to do in this operation is sign the hotel register, get in a pair of pajamas, and—the only hard part—look surprised when your picture is taken.
MACKELWAINE. (*Indicating the package.*) I brought my pajamas. It's a good thing I remembered.

BARBEE. Miss Bagley'll have pajamas for you.
MACKELWAINE. No kidding?
BARBEE. She takes care of everything. She supplies the pajamas, the house detective, the photographer and three glossy prints. All for two hundred dollars. It's called a package deal. (*Helen enters with the drink.*)
HELEN. Here you are, Mister MacKelwaine.
MACKELWAINE. Thank you, Miss Foster. (*To Barbee.*) Who takes the picture?
BARBEE. What picture?
MACKELWAINE. The photograph of Miss Bagley and me in bed?
BARBEE. Well, it might rain, but on the other hand it might not.
MACKELWAINE. (*Puzzled.*) Huh?
BARBEE. It's been cloudy all day. It's hard to tell.
MACKELWAINE. What's the matter with you?
HELEN. (*Smiling.*) If your lawyer knows you're a co-respondent it's called "collusion." Mister Barbee doesn't know what you're talking about.
MACKELWAINE. He's the one been talking about it!
HELEN. Not in front of a witness.
MACKELWAINE. Oh. I see. (*He looks at Barbee, who smiles at him.*) Lawyers! (*Helen takes her purse, and starts out.*)
HELEN. See you at eight o'clock, Mister MacKelwaine. Don't be nervous, we've never lost a husband yet.
BARBEE. Take it easy with the accountant!
HELEN. (*At the door. Mock dignity.*) "How dare you address me in a public elevator, sir!" At least he'll know to enter the five dollars in his debit column. (*She's out.*)
MACKELWAINE. What was that?
BARBEE. Private joke.
MACKELWAINE. You making time with that girl?
BARBEE. Are you crazy?
MACKELWAINE. Think she'd go out with me?
BARBEE. I hope not! I thought you were through with women.
MACKELWAINE. Who said that?
BARBEE. You did. You spent two hours in the Turkish Baths telling me you were going to be operated on and become a eunuch.
MACKELWAINE. Well, I did.
BARBEE. (*Startled.*) You had the operation?

MacKELWAINE. (*He nods.*) Yep. It didn't take. (*He drinks, Barbee eyes him. The lights go out.*)

ACT I

Scene 2

The stage turns to reveal the interior of an elevator. We see three walls, the door being left to our imagination. Helen faces front. Appropriate sound, and the movement of the shaft, visible beyond the rear grill, simulate motion. The elevator halts. From the darkness steps Woodrow W. O'Malley, into the elevator.
Woodrow is twenty-seven, quite attractive, a courteous, upstanding, intelligent young man. Helen is to his right, and slightly to his rear. She looks at him, relaxed. The elevator stops.

WOODROW. (*Only fair play-acting.*) Say! What's happened? (*He looks to Helen, who remains expressionless. He presses a button on the panel.*) That's funny. (*He turns to Helen.*) Don't get frightened now, there's nothing to be alarmed about. (*Helen just returns his look.*) I'll have you out of here in no time. (*He takes the telephone from its stand and presses the call button.*) Hello, hello! . . . (*To Helen.*) I'm sure it's a temporary power shortage. Or maybe a fuse, that's all. Calm, now. (*Helen looks at her wrist watch.*)
TOM'S VOICE. (*Through the telephone.*) Hello?
WOODROW. Hello! We're stuck in the elevator! Between the sixth and fifth floors!
TOM'S VOICE. Nothing to worry about! Must be a fuse! I'll have you moving in two minutes!
WOODROW. Okay. (*Tom clicks off, Woodrow hangs up.*) There you are! Nothing to it! (*He looks hopefully to Helen and smiles.*) I must say I admire your aplomb.
HELEN. (*Flat.*) My what?
WOODROW. Your aplomb. Your poise. Some girls might scream.
HELEN. (*Flat.*) I'm not the screaming type.
WOODROW. (*An inch taken aback.*) No, I guess you're not.

(*Another tack.*) I've noticed you in this elevator before. I didn't think you were that type. (*No encouragement in Helen's expression.*) My name is Woody O'Malley. (*He waits for Helen to introduce herself. She looks at him and says nothing. Now she looks at her watch, and keeps looking at it.*) Woody is for Woodrow, and Woodrow, as you may suspect, is for Woodrow Wilson. My father was a great admirer of Wilson's. (*He is having trouble sustaining his confidence.*) He thought the failure of the League of Nations was one of the world's great tragedies. I think so too. (*No response.*) You're not very interested in politics?
HELEN. (*Polite, but stand-offish.*) No, I'm not.
WOODROW. (*A determined effort.*) I hope you don't think me too forward, but—since this opportunity presented itself—may I ask you to dinner this evening?
HELEN. I'm awfully sorry. I have a dinner engagement. (*He would say something, she anticipates.*) And tomorrow evening.
WOODROW. (*He knows when he's licked.*) Well, you can't rule a fellow out for trying.
HELEN. (*She gives him this much.*) No, you can't.
WOODROW. No hard feelings, I hope.
HELEN. Not at all. (*A pause.*)
WOODROW. I thought it needed dinner to explain it all, but maybe I can manage here. You see, I know you're a legal secretary—I asked—and I thought maybe you—or perhaps somebody you know who does the same type of work—might be interested in taking a similar job in Paris?
HELEN. What's that?
WOODROW. I'm looking for a secretary who's had legal training to work in Paris.
HELEN. Paris, France?
WOODROW. Why, yes. Is there another?
HELEN. (*Thinking furiously.*) There's one in Kentucky.
WOODROW. No, I mean the one in France. (*The elevator starts, with sound.*)
HELEN. (*Looking at the moving grill.*) Oh damn!
WOODROW. (*Surprised and puzzled at her reaction.*) What's the matter? (*She looks at him sharply.*)
HELEN. Is this on the level, or is this a more complicated pitch?
WOODROW. Pitch?
HELEN. To have a date with me?

WOODROW. It's on the level. I've been appointed in charge of our Paris office and I'm looking for a legal secretary.
HELEN. (*She looks at him a long moment, and decides to chance it.*) Where are we having dinner?
WOODROW. What happened to your date?
HELEN. I haven't any. I made it up. (*The elevator stops.*)
WOODROW. (*A grin.*) Why, you told a lie!
HELEN. People who pay five dollars to stop elevators shouldn't throw stones! (*She steps out into the darkness, Woodrow follows, surprised. Lights go out.*)

ACT I

Scene 3

Lights come up again on the booth of a small French-type restaurant.
Helen and Woodrow are just slipping into their seats, still looking the place over.

HELEN. How did you find this restaurant?
WOODROW. In the Yellow Pages of the Telephone Directory. Under French restaurants. I figure I can practice my French while I'm ordering. You don't mind French food, I hope.
HELEN. I like it.
WOODROW. "The national genius of the French is their cuisine." I read that someplace and I believe it. (*He practices, in halting syllables.*) Qu'est-ce que recommendez-vous, s'il vous plait? That's "What do you recommend, please?" I think I got it right, the "vous" comes after the "recommendez" because it's a question. (*He sees the waiter approaching.*) Here goes. (*The waiter enters the scene. He is in very good spirits.*)
WAITER. Bonjour.
WOODROW. Bonjour. (*Trying to carry it off.*) Qu'est-ce que recommendez-vous, s'il vous plait? (*The waiter now merely looks at him.*) No, eh? I'll try it more nasal, that's what the book says. Qu'est-ce que recommendez-vous, s'il vous plait?
WAITER. (*Smiling, no accent at all.*) You want to speak French?

WOODROW. (*Grinning at him.*) I'm trying to learn. You don't mind my practising?
WAITER. Not at all. But I don't know what the hell you're talking about. (*To Helen with a smile.*) Pardon the language.
HELEN. (*Delighted.*) Perfectly all right.
WOODROW. You mean you don't speak French?
WAITER. Not a word.
WOODROW. What about "Bonjour"?
WAITER. Say, that's right. I forgot. Well, I speak one word.
WOODROW. It's two words!
WAITER. No kidding. I speak two words! I'm going to ask my brother-in-law for a raise! He owns the place. This is his idea, if I say "Bonjour" to the customers it'll make the place seem Frenchy. What do you think?
WOODROW. Well, it fooled me. What happens if a real Frenchman comes in?
WAITER. It happened once. One of the busboys speaks French and we put 'em together. They got into a fight over De Gaulle.
WOODROW. (*Looking at the menu.*) What's "Pot au feu"?
WAITER. You ever eat at Lindy's?
WOODROW. Uh huh.
WAITER. It's like their "Chicken in the pot." But not as good.
WOODROW. (*Amused at his honesty.*) If it's not as good why should I eat it here?
WAITER. You're here already, we have to make a living too, eat it, it won't kill you.
WOODROW. (*To Helen.*) Suit you?
HELEN. Fine.
WOODROW. (*He holds up two fingers.*) Doo pots au feu.
WAITER. It's good you got fingers. (*He writes it on his pad as he goes.*)
WOODROW. Character! Well, what shall we talk about? Pick a subject.
HELEN. The subject is the job in Paris!
WOODROW. Ah yes, that subject.
HELEN. (*Again.*) There *is* such a job? Or you'll be eating two chickens in the pot!
WOODROW. You're the most suspicious girl I've ever met.
HELEN. That's right. Tell me about the job.
WOODROW. Legal secretary. Just like the job you have. In

Paris. Very reliable firm. We pay two way transportation, economy class fare. You are obliged to stay six months, otherwise you pay your own return. You'll love it.
HELEN. Hold it. You've left something out.
WOODROW. Yes, you'll be my personal, private secretary.
HELEN. The salary!
WOODROW. (*Slightly apprehensive.*) Sixty dollars a week.
HELEN. Sixty dollars! Why, I make almost double that!
WOODROW. (*Truly concerned.*) Do you really?
HELEN. I'll show you my salary check! You'd have to pay me at least a hundred. That is, if I took the job.
WOODROW. It's out of the question. The thing works by a Table of Organization, that's what the job's pencilled in for.
HELEN. Pencil it out! Write in a larger number!
WOODROW. The company doesn't work like that.
HELEN. Well, I couldn't live on that salary, it'd be absolutely impossible.
WOODROW. (*Hopefully but without confidence.*) Money goes further in Europe.
HELEN. It couldn't go that far.
WOODROW. Rents are cheaper, transportation, clothes—
HELEN. You mean I can buy Dior dresses on sixty dollars a week?
WOODROW. Food wouldn't be an item. You'd be having dinner with me.
HELEN. I may want to skip one evening.
WOODROW. You're making a big mistake. (*Persuasively.*) Have you ever been to Paris? (*She shakes her head.*) What they tell you about the light is true. It's a kind of blue haze. It settles over everything, the chestnut trees, the old buildings, the gendarmes. There's no street in the world like the Champs Elysees, the Arch of Triumph's right in the middle of it. The street lamps of the Place de la Concorde are still gas lit, they tried to change them to electricity and the National Assembly passed a law forbidding it! At night we go to St. Germain, the artists' quarter. We eat outside at little tables with the students. You'll meet people who've come from all over the world; from India, Scandinavia, Japan, South America, all commingling in one giant forum of contrasting cultures and viewpoints. And do they argue! And anybody can join in! France has two hours for lunch, a five day week and lots of holidays! There are trips to be taken, in a two by four automobile,

on which I've already put a deposit. Don't you want to see Rome, Florence, Pisa, the Cote d'Azur, Copenhagen, Capri, Salzburg and Portofino? (*A rising plea.*) For heaven's sake, aren't you tired of Jones Beach?

HELEN. (*After a pause.*) I'll take ninety dollars. Not a penny less.

WOODROW. The Table of Organization says sixty.

HELEN. I send forty dollars home to my mother.

WOODROW. Oh, oh! Even with me feeding you dinner you couldn't make it. (*He thinks.*) You wouldn't think of marrying me, would you? I need a secretary badly.

HELEN. One of these days, bucko, that little gambit is going to get you in trouble.

WOODROW. I'm safe. I knew you wouldn't take me up on it. (*He eyes her.*) Still, you're my type. I always like girls that look like you, and you look more like you than anyone I ever met.

HELEN. Why won't your company pay the going rate for a legal secretary?

WOODROW. They don't even want me to hire an American girl. All this is my idea! I'm lucky they'll pay your fare!

HELEN. You're trying to exploit cheap foreign labour. Me!

WOODROW. (*Unhappily.*) That's the size of it.

HELEN. Well, thanks for the offer anyway. (*They reflect, depressed. The waiter appears with the tray of two tureens. He puts them down, looking at both their faces.*)

WAITER. What are you so unhappy about, you haven't even tasted it yet!

WOODROW. It's not the food.

WAITER. A fight, eh? Never argue on an empty stomach! In my house I have a rule. I don't talk until I've finished eating. That's *my* rule. My wife has her own rules. Eat up, kids. (*He leaves. Woodrow takes his spoon.*)

HELEN. Do I still get the "Chicken in the pot"?

WOODROW. You can have mine, too. I've lost my appetite.

HELEN. (*Tasting the soup.*) It's good. Go on, begin. (*He does.*)

WOODROW Pity we haven't got the guts to get married. Probably work out fine. A lot of being happily married is luck, you know. People don't act the same when they're courting as when they're married. You've got to jump in to find out.

HELEN. Might be too late then. A ten minute acquaintanceship is a little short.
WOODROW. What about the three weeks in the elevator?
HELEN. Well, adding up all the elevator time would only come to another half hour at the most. Still not enough. (*They eat two spoonfuls of soup in silence.*) I'd like to review the situation.
WOODROW. Shoot.
HELEN. First, there is such a job?
WOODROW. (*Indignant.*) What's the matter with you?
HELEN. Second, I only have to stay six months? To get my return fare?
WOODROW. You'll be crazy about me before six months. You won't want to leave.
HELEN. That brings up the personal note. This kind of talk is all right in restaurants, but the personal, private secretary part and those trips to Pisa and Portofino ring a bell. What, exactly, would my duties be if I took the job—I'm not saying I'll take it—and I mean all my duties?
WOODROW. (*Leaning forward.*) All your duties are confined to the office and get your mind out of the gutter.
HELEN. Gladly.
WOODROW. I've told you the attractive part of the job, you might as well hear the unpleasant part.
HELEN. This is the time for it.
WOODROW. Office hours are eight—eight, I said—a.m., to six p.m. Those are French hours, we conform. It is not a job with much leisure to it, I'm understaffed, you'll have a lot of work.
HELEN. I don't mind the work.
WOODROW. All this love-making that's going on now won't go on in the office. Sorry, but necessary.
HELEN. You're listing that under the unpleasant part?
WOODROW. (*Keeps eating.*) Uh huh. But after hours, I'll keep up a campaign that'll knock you off your feet. (*She looks at him sharply, not knowing how he meant it. He didn't mean it with any implication.*) That just came out that way. Better send for your passport.
HELEN. I haven't decided to take the job yet.
WOODROW. And you have to give notice about the job you have now.

HELEN. In the first place, I'd have to borrow the money to send home to my mother. I'd need a thousand dollars.
WOODROW. We leave in three weeks.
HELEN. And I'm not sure I can get it.
WOODROW. I'll book your plane reservation.
HELEN. I'd want a contract, with the six months return fare written in it.
WOODROW. We seem to be all settled!
HELEN. (*Eyeing.*) You have remarkable capacity for not hearing what you don't want to hear.
WOODROW. (*Beaming at her.*) What shall we do after dinner? How about ice hockey? I mean see it, not play it. There's a good game at the Garden.
HELEN. I have a chore at eight o'clock. And after that I have to call my uncle in Chicago about the thousand dollars.
WOODROW. What kind of chore?
HELEN. (*Deliberately.*) A personal matter! I'll tell you tomorrow if I'm able to go. I'm not sure my uncle'll give me the money. Although when he sees me he always pinches me.
WOODROW. That's a good sign.
HELEN. When I was tiny my nickname was Penny. That was when he started the pinching. He said he was my penny pinching uncle.
WOODROW. (*He eyes her in mock solemnity.*) This—comic strain—I trust is not hereditary and our children will be free from the taint? (*They exchange looks a moment.*)
HELEN. I'll be frank with you. If I take the job I'll do my work faithfully but I'm only interested in seeing Europe. I'll leave after six months.
WOODROW. You especially encumbered by any fiance or such impediment?
HELEN. I have a number of admirers.
WOODROW. Including me. Anybody indispensable?
HELEN. (*She shakes her head, smiles.*) Nobody. Including you.
WOODROW. A temporary condition. (*Never stopping his eating, he reaches in his pocket and extracts a small package which he puts beside her plate.*) A present.
HELEN. What is it?
WOODROW. Perfume. Blue Hour.

HELEN. How did you know I use it?
WOODROW. I've been sniffing you in the elevator for three weeks! I had a hell of a job in the store sniffing all those bottles until I hit the right one. I came out smelling like a madam in a— (*He changes his mind about using the phrase.*) That smell sticks with you, everyone in the subway kept looking at me! A sailor winked at me!
HELEN. (*Looking at him.*) You certainly are a peculiar fellow.
WOODROW. That's what the sailor thought. He was wrong. (*She eats, looking at him. He eats, looking at her, smiling. Lights out.*)

ACT I

SCENE 4

The lights come on and we are in Room 1640 of the Mansvoort Hotel.
R. *is a desk and typewriter,* L. *a Murphy bed, now concealed. Doors are* R. C., *to the bathroom and* U. C., *to the corridor. New York night skyline through the windows. Present are Barbee and MacKelwaine, and two newcomers, Butch Flowers and Joey Hallop.*
Butch is a forty-year-old ex-prizefighter; Joey, in bellhop uniform, is small and quick. Joey's camera is beside him, Butch's derby beside the camera. They are playing gin rummy.
Barbee and MacKelwaine sit, the former reading a newspaper, the latter thinking his thoughts, his legs crossed. which he uncrosses in his nervousness. This tableau has been going on for quite a while.

JOEY. (*Picking up a card, considering it, and then throwing it down forcefully.*) Here! Take it!
BUTCH. (*He picks up another card.*) I don't want it.
JOEY. What do you mean, you don't want it, it's a nine! You picked up two nines! You gotta want it!
BUTCH. It's a law? I don't want it!
JOEY. You sure you know how to play gin rummy?

BUTCH. (*Pointing to the score card.*) I've blitzed you twice and you're telling me how to play?
JOEY. Shoot. (*Butch discards a card, they continue playing.*)
MacKELWAINE. (*Poking his chest.*) That lobster I ate's lying right here. And kicking. (*Looking at his watch.*) Shouldn't this Bagley woman be here by now?
BARBEE. (*Reading the paper.*) She'll be here.
MacKELWAINE. Well, she's late.
BARBEE. Don't be nervous.
MacKELWAINE. I've got to catch a train.
BARBEE. Tonight? For where?
MacKELWAINE. (*Hesitantly.*) Atlantic City.
BARBEE. (*He nods knowingly.*) Isn't it a little early for that?
MacKELWAINE. What do you want me to do, take up knitting?
BARBEE. How about cold baths?
MacKELWAINE. (*Sarcasm.*) Funeee!
BARBEE. (*To create a diversion.*) MacKelwaine, do you know who this man is?
MacKELWAINE. (*Looking to the indicated Butch.*) He's the house detective.
BARBEE. Before he was a house detective he fought for the middle weight championship of the world.
JOEY. (*Still in the cards.*) He lost!
BUTCH. Play cards!
MacKELWAINE. What name did he fight under?
BARBEE. Butch Flowers. Did you ever see him?
MacKELWAINE. (*Thinking.*) I remember a Tiger Flowers. (*Recalling.*) But he was colored.
JOEY. *He* used to be colored.
BUTCH. One of these days I'm going to hit you on top of the head and drive you into the floor like a carpet tack.
JOEY. You lay one hand on me and it's a felony. (*To Barbee.*) Isn't that right, counsellor, a professional fighter who hits anyone is the same as someone else using a gun?
BARBEE. That's right, Joey.
JOEY. Tell you what, Butch, as long as it's the law, I'll fight you like that. You wear boxing gloves and I'll use a gun.
BUTCH. (*Eyeing him.*) It appeals to me! Let me think about it! (*The door opens, Helen appears.*)

HELEN. (*Indicating the door.*) It says "Public Stenographer." I thought I had the wrong room. I'm sorry I'm late.
BARBEE. That's all right, Miss Bagley hasn't shown up yet. (*To Butch and Joey.*) Would you boys mind stepping out in the hall for a moment?
JOEY. Okay, counsellor.
BUTCH. (*Taking it.*) I'll hold the score.
JOEY. (*Leaving.*) Don't you trust me?
BUTCH. Not for ninety cents! (*They're out.*)
BARBEE. (*Taking the property settlement out of his pocket.*) Notarize the three copies. (*Helen seats herself, takes out her seal and fountain pen and will perform the operation. MacKelwaine goes to the phone. Barbee resumes reading the newspaper.*)
MACKELWAINE. Operator, Circle 7-4131 . . . (*To Barbee.*) I can't miss that train . . . (*Into phone.*) Marilyn? (*Barbee looks toward him, MacKelwaine is uncomfortable at the exposure and turns his back to him.*) I'm still in this business conference . . . You're all packed, aren't you? (*Lower.*) Would I take you to Atlantic City if I didn't love you . . .
BARBEE. (*Reflectively.*) That'd make a good song title. It's touching.
MACKELWAINE. (*Into phone, wanting to get off.*) We'll talk about it in Atlantic City!
BARBEE. That's good too.
MACKELWAINE. Now, Marilyn, don't say that. I've been thinking about you night and day.
BARBEE. That one's been used.
MACKELWAINE. Honey, I'll call you back from another phone! (*He hangs up and starts out.*) She heard you, stupid!
BARBEE. (*During his cross.*) I was making background noises, like a business conference. (*MacKelwaine slams the door after himself.*) Would you believe he's a successful businessman? A regular tycoon. Doesn't seem to be any connection between the top and bottom half of a man.
HELEN. (*Having finished.*) All done. (*She folds them up and hands them to Barbee, who puts them in his inside pocket.*)
BARBEE. Thank you, Helen. Take one hair wash out of petty cash.
HELEN. Thank you, I will.
BARBEE. What happened in the elevator? Anything unpleasant?

HELEN. No.
BARBEE. Did the accountant ask you to dinner?
HELEN. Uh huh.
BARBEE. Was he put out when you wouldn't go?
HELEN. No, because I went.
BARBEE. You went to dinner with him?
HELEN. Uh huh.
BARBEE. I'm surprised.
HELEN. I am, too. He's offered me a job in Paris.
BARBEE. Hey!
HELEN. He offered to marry me, too, but he wasn't on the level about that. I hope he is about the job.
BARBEE. Now look here, Helen, I hope you're too smart a girl to be taken in by some operator!
HELEN. Oh, I'll investigate him. The job doesn't pay much and I had to borrow a thousand from my uncle in Chicago to make ends meet. That's why I was late.
BARBEE. I'll be damned. You mean I had a secretary before dinner and now I haven't?
HELEN. I want to see Paris, Mister Barbee. In that blue light.
BARBEE. What blue light?
HELEN. I'm not sure, but I want to see it awfully bad. Before I settle down in those three rooms and a play pen.
BARBEE. (*A moment.*) Are you interested in this young man? Personally?
HELEN. You mean real interested? "Play pen" interested?
BARBEE. Uh huh.
HELEN. (*Doubtfully.*) I don't think so. He's— (*Groping.*)—a little too quick for me. I'm afraid I couldn't manage him. He's not really my type. He says I'm his, though.
BARBEE. Far away from your mother—in Paris—under all that blue light, your type might change.
HELEN. It's a risk a girl has to take.
BARBEE. I had a feeling I shouldn't have let you get in that elevator. (*The door opens and MacKelwaine, Butch and Joey enter.*)
MACKELWAINE. (*Observing no Bagley.*) Isn't she here yet? (*He looks at his watch.*) I've got to get out of here!
BUTCH. She's never been late before.
JOEY. Never. She once showed up doubled over with appendicitis.

While the ambulance was on the way she posed for the picture. You remember that, Butch?
BUTCH. Yeah. She says it's like she's on the stage and the show has to go on. She feels she's in a type of show business, only she acts for a very small audience.
JOEY. (*Concerned.*) I hope she hasn't had an accident. (*He knocks wood.*)
BUTCH. (*He does too.*) Me neither.
MACKELWAINE. I can't stay here much longer! (*Barbee, lost in thought, turns slowly toward Helen, contemplating her. All turn to her.*)
BARBEE. Want to make a hundred dollars?
HELEN. Doing what? (*She gets it.*) Are you serious?
BARBEE. There's nothing to it.
HELEN. (*Indignant.*) Of course not!
BARBEE. No one sees your face, and you don't take your clothes off.
HELEN. Certainly not! What's the matter with you?
BUTCH. (*Enacting it.*) You just get in bed and stick one arm out in front of your face, and Joey snaps your picture.
JOEY. Nobody'd recognize you, lady! Unless you're tattooed!
MACKELWAINE. Please, Miss Foster! I'd appreciate it!
BARBEE. I'm staying in the room, Helen. (*She seems to be wavering.*) Helen, would I let you do it if it wasn't all right?
HELEN. What would I have to do?
BARBEE. Just pose with a bare shoulder. Half a shoulder'll do.
JOEY. (*Taking his camera.*) I'll shoot a low angle! You won't see nothing!
BARBEE. What are you wearing under that?
HELEN. A slip.
BARBEE. Take your dress off. (*Helen is undecided.*) For heaven's sake, you wear a bathing suit in public!
HELEN. It's not the same.
BUTCH. (*To MacKelwaine.*) Slip that coat off, sir, and step over here! (*Butch opens the closet door, exhibiting a row of pajama tops on hangers. He selects one.*) This ought to be your size. You like green?
MACKELWAINE. It's not my favorite color.
JOEY. It's a black and white picture!

BUTCH. Always keep the customer happy! (*He offers a lavender striped number.*) How's this?
MACKELWAINE. I'll take the green!
BUTCH. (*Obliging.*) Okay! (*Barbee goes to the bed, and pulls the blanket back.*)
BARBEE. Come on, Helen, let's get it over with! (*Helen, quite ill at ease, starts to unbutton her dress. She looks to Butch, who watches her while MacKelwaine is changing.*)
BUTCH. I'm a married man, miss, I got five kids. (*She looks to Joey.*)
JOEY. I'm like a doctor.
BUTCH. (*Surveying the fit on MacKelwaine.*) Like it was made to order for you. But you better take your tie off. (*Helen has her dress off, but holds it in front of her.*)
BARBEE. Get in bed, Helen! Don't be silly about it! (*Helen throws the dress on the bed and quickly dodges under the blanket. Barbee goes to the dress and takes it.*)
HELEN. (*Alarmed.*) Where are you taking my dress?
BARBEE. Out of the photograph! (*He now rolls MacKelwaine's shirt collar further down so that it doesn't appear over the pajama top.*) All right, get in! (*MacKelwaine gets in bed, Helen retreats to the far side.*) Now put your hand up, like this! Like you've been surprised and you're hiding your face! (*Helen pulls the blanket over herself entirely.*) Come on out! (*He uncovers the head and shoulders.*) What's the matter with you?
JOEY. (*After looking through the finder.*) This ain't a wide angle lens, lady. Can't you get a little closer? (*Helen looks to Barbee.*)
BARBEE. Lean toward him a little. (*She doesn't.*) Helen! (*MacKelwaine moves closer to her. He assumes a surprised pose.*)
JOEY. Watch the birdie! One—two—three! (*He snaps the photoflash.*) There you are!
BARBEE. You sure you got it?
JOEY. (*Indignant.*) Certainly!
BARBEE. We could take another to be safe?
JOEY. I ain't missed one in five years!
BARBEE. (*Throwing Helen the dress, MacKelwaine the shirt.*) Get dressed! Didn't hurt, did it?
HELEN. (*Smiling.*) No.
MACKELWAINE. I'm much obliged, Miss Foster.
BUTCH. We've left something out! (*All look to him.*)

BARBEE. What?
BUTCH. My part!
BARBEE. Oh yes! (*He takes the shirt and dress from them.*) I forgot. Miss Bagley usually stages all this!
HELEN. I thought this was all!
BARBEE. Nothing to it! Just lie there! (*To Butch.*) Go on! Do it! (*Butch goes to the door.*) You don't have to go out the door!
BUTCH. I know my job, Mister Barbee. (*He goes out.*)
JOEY. He likes to do it right. (*Butch comes into the room, closing the door behind him.*)
BUTCH. I see you, Mister MacKelwaine, in bed with a woman! (*To Barbee.*) That's it.
BARBEE. Fine! (*He throws the shirt and dress to the bedfellows, who will hastily dress. Barbee takes a money clip from his pocket and peels off bills.*) That's twenty-five each, isn't it? (*He gives them the money.*)
BUTCH. Thank you, Mister Barbee.
BARBEE. That's not my name, you don't know who I am.
BUTCH. Okay.
JOEY. (*Taking the bills.*) Thank you, Mister—. Thank you.
BARBEE. (*To Butch.*) How does the room get paid for?
BUTCH. Miss Bagley rents it by the month. She charges clients twenty-five dollars per use.
BARBEE. Per use! Couldn't be fairer! (*Giving him the money.*) Give it to her when you see her.
BUTCH. Yes sir.
BARBEE. (*To Joey.*) Three glossy prints. To my office.
JOEY. Bring 'em myself.
BARBEE. (*Dismissing them.*) Thank you, boys.
JOEY. You're welcome.
BUTCH. Much obliged. Sorry about Miss Bagley, something must have happened to her. (*They start to leave. To the others.*) Nice to have met you.
JOEY. Likewise. (*An after-thought at the door.*) You want a print for yourself, miss? On the house?
HELEN. No thanks.
JOEY. Well, goodbye.
MACKELWAINE. Goodbye.
HELEN. Goodbye. (*They exit. Barbee peels two more bills off.*)

BARBEE. (*Giving them to Helen.*) Fifty—one hundred. If you ever made an easier one hundred dollars tell me about it.
HELEN. (*Looking at the money.*) You really don't have to pay me—
BARBEE. Take it! (*To MacKelwaine.*) She really ought to get a hundred and twenty-five! That's what Bagley would net.
MACKELWAINE. (*Agreeing.*) Spend my money!
BARBEE. (*Counting out the additional money.*) Ten—twenty—five!
HELEN. My goodness, a hundred dollars is quite enough!
BARBEE. Mind your business! That's the union rate! You don't want to be a scab, do you?
HELEN. (*A smile, frankly.*) No.
MACKELWAINE. (*Hurrying his coat on.*) Well, I hate to kiss and run—I'm really not that type—but I've got a train to catch. Thank you again, Miss Foster, for your—services.
HELEN. Thank *you*, Mister MacKelwaine.
MACKELWAINE. Counsellor. Good day. (*He starts.*)
BARBEE. So long. Bring me back some salt water taffy.
MACKELWAINE. (*At the door.*) If I get to the boardwalk. (*He's out.*)
BARBEE. Goat! Well, young lady, what are you thinking?
HELEN. If my mother knew!
BARBEE. (*Going for his own hat.*) Don't tell her.
HELEN. Is this how it's always done?
BARBEE. About.
HELEN. It's not very honest.
BARBEE. No, just legal.
HELEN. Aren't honest and legal slightly similar?
BARBEE. Only in the dictionary. The divorce laws in this state have made us liars and hypocrites, I am ashamed to say. Very ashamed, for my profession and myself. (*He goes to the door.*) Good night, Helen.
HELEN. Are you going to tell Mrs. Barbee about this?
BARBEE. If you don't want me to I won't.
HELEN. If you gave me your word now that you wouldn't tell, would you still tell her? (*He smiles at her and nods. She smiles at him.*) That's the way it should be. Good night, Mister Barbee. (*He's out. Helen goes to her purse, takes out her make-up, and sits in front of the dressing table mirror. She works on her face a*

moment, and the door opens, admitting a large breathless woman—Miss Gladys Bagley. She is about thirty, a good-natured, over-blown, over-dyed blonde. She has had a bit too much to drink.)

GLADYS. (*Seeing only Helen.*) Hey! Where's everybody!

HELEN. Are you Miss Bagley?

GLADYS. Yep! Who are you?

HELEN. I'm Mister Barbee's secretary, Miss Foster. We've spoken on the phone.

GLADYS. Yeah. Miss Foster! Hi ya, kid. Everybody blow?

HELEN. Yes, they've gone.

GLADYS. Hell, I'm sorry! I never had that happen before! I wonder what I ought to do? Think I ought to call 'em up?

HELEN. (*Hesitantly.*) Well—we took the picture—

GLADYS. You did?

HELEN. Yes, with me. Mister MacKelwaine had to catch a train. I hope that's all right.

GLADYS. (*Relieved.*) Certainly it's all right.

HELEN. (*Going for her purse.*) You can have the money—

GLADYS. Forget it!

HELEN. Well, let's go half. That would be fair.

GLADYS. (*She laughs loosely.*) Buy yourself a hanky with it, kid. (*She flops into a chair.*) I gotta sit, I'm bushed! (*She winks.*) I ain't bushed so much as cock-eyed! I'm celebrating!

HELEN. Really?

GLADYS. I'm gettin' married! Can you beat it?

HELEN. Well, that's very nice.

GLADYS. Who'd ever thought I'd go for the rice and old shoes! I can't get over it! I must be out of my mind!

HELEN. (*Smiling.*) You're probably just in love.

GLADYS. Oh, I'm in love all right, but I'm also out of my mind! With what I know about marriage, in this line of work, for me to still want to try it—I tell you I ought to be locked up! (*She wets her lip.*) I'm a little drunk.

HELEN. You're only exuberant.

GLADYS. Drunk, too. (*She thinks a moment.*) Lawdy, I love that man. You know where I met him? (*She points to the bed and nods.*) Right there. A client.

HELEN. (*More to be courteous.*) Really?

GLADYS. (*Over-nodding.*) He asked me to go out with him. I

said "no." I never go out with any of them. In this line of work you have to keep your nose clean. You start going with the brand new ex-husbands, all of 'em busting out of marriage like a steer coming out of a rodeo chute—you aren't going to be in the co-respondent business long. You're going to be in another kind of business, you know what I mean? (*Helen nods. Gladys raises her hand.*) In six years, can you imagine how many husbands in that bed, not one laid a hand on me. Or vice versa.
HELEN. That's commendable.
GLADYS. (*Suspiciously.*) What's that?
HELEN. I said that's to be admired.
GLADYS. Well, I figured it was the business I was in. If I met them as clients I wouldn't date them. That was my rule. And then Charlie came along. Boy, he bugs me. And the funny thing is I didn't think he was much when I first saw him. Just another client. I put the pajamas on him—he started to laugh—he's got the whitest teeth—I said "What's funny?" He said "I've never worn pajamas over my clothes." I said, "You ever had your picture taken in bed with a woman?" He said, "No, but if I have to begin I'm happy to begin with you." And he smiled. With those white teeth. That did it. Maybe my resistance was low, I'd just gotten over the flu, I don't know, but in any case, we've been seeing each other for a month, and I wake up smiling. Laughing sometimes!
HELEN. Good for you! Where are you going for your honeymoon?
GLADYS. We been on our honeymoon, now we're going to get married.
HELEN. (*Taken aback.*) Oh.
GLADYS. Couldn't be helped. The poor guy was being robbed by that wife of his. She kept raising the alimony. Every time he agreed, she'd raise it again. She gave him ulcers. He has to take a pill every four hours. I tell you he's a saint. Never heard a word out of him.
HELEN. (*She gets up to go.*) Well, I hope it works out—
GLADYS. Oh, it's all settled now. We're off to Mexico to get married. That's how I got caught drunk. Drinking tequila! Wahoo! No wonder they have revolutions! (*The door opens, admitting Butch.*)
BUTCH. Where you been, we been worried about you!

GLADYS. Thanks for the worrying, Butch. I was in good hands, I was with my future husband.
BUTCH. You're marrying that Patterson fellow?
GLADYS. God help him! We're off for Mexico City tomorrow morning! Mrs. Charlie Patterson! That's me!
HELEN. (*Trying to go.*) Well, lots of luck. (*They are arrested by a loud buzzing. Helen and Butch are startled.*)
BUTCH. What's that?
GLADYS. That's me! (*She pulls her sleeve up to reveal a wrist watch, the type with alarm. She presses the button which stops the ringing.*) It's a wrist watch with an alarm! I bought it for a wedding present for Charlie! I'm not taking any chance Charlie's going to sleep past that plane time! And it'll tell him when to take his ulcer pill.
BUTCH. Why did it go off now?
GLADYS. Beats me. I must've set it. But what for? (*She stares at the watch.*) What's supposed to happen right now at half past eight? (*The door opens and a short, diffident man enters. His name is Alexander Brown.*)
BROWN. My name is Alexander Brown. I was told to be here at half past eight.
GLADYS. Jumpin' catfish! Another client! That's what I set it for! What's the matter with me! We're doing a double header today! (*She goes, slightly unsteady, to Brown, while Helen hurries to her purse on the dressing table preparatory to leaving.*) Come right in, Mister Brown. You're from the Kendall office, aren't you?
BROWN. Yes.
GLADYS. (*She starts to unbutton his coat, to his surprise.*) We're kinda discomboombelated today, Mister Brown, but we'll take care of you fine! Butch, get Joey!
BUTCH. (*Rushing out.*) Right!
GLADYS. (*Still unbuttoning Brown, to Helen, who is crossing to exit.*) Get him a pajama coat! Size D! (*Helen hesitates, preferring to leave, feels obliged to perform this small courtesy. She puts her purse down and goes to the closet and will find the coat.*)
BROWN. This won't take long, will it?
GLADYS. Two shakes of a lamb's tail! Take your tie off, Mister Brown! (*He starts on his belt.*) Just your tie, Mister Brown.
BROWN. I'm a little nervous.
GLADYS. That's perfectly normal.

BROWN. I registered as Mister Brown and the clerk didn't believe it was my real name.
GLADYS. (*Occupied in her work.*) He's a very suspicious man. (*She takes the coat from Helen.*) Go on, take your dress off and jump in the hay!
HELEN. Me?
GLADYS. If I lie down I won't be able to get up again! (*Helen, reluctant, cannot think of an alternative and starts to take her dress off again. Gladys fits the coat on to Mister Brown and helps him button up.*)
BROWN. This is very strange to me.
GLADYS. It's strange to everybody, Mister Brown. (*She holds him by the arm, escorting him to the bed.*) In we go! Beddy-bye! (*Mister Brown is quite shy. Gladys adjusts the blanket, lifts up Helen's arm to cover her face.*) Like that, dear. Shoulder out! Let the judge get a look at it! He's got to see at least a shoulder! (*She adjusts Brown's face to look front, surveys all, steps back out of camera vision and calls.*) Okay, Butch! (*The door bursts open, admitting Butch and Joey behind him, camera at the ready.*)
BUTCH. I see you, Mister Brown, in bed with a woman!
JOEY. Watch the birdie! One—two—three. (*He snaps the picture.*)
GLADYS. (*To Brown.*) There you are, Mister Brown! (*To Helen.*) Put your dress on! (*Helen does. To Brown.*) That was nothing to be nervous about. Didn't hurt a bit, did it?
BROWN. (*Happy now.*) No, it didn't.
GLADYS. (*To Joey.*) Three glossies to the Kendall office.
JOEY. Right. We thought you had an accident!
GLADYS. I don't have accidents, Joey. You know that. That's two hundred dollars, Mister Brown.
BROWN. (*In the midst of the coat buttoning.*) Certainly. (*He takes out his wallet and counts out the money.*) Four fifties, that all right?
GLADYS. They're the right color. (*She hands one of the bills to Butch.*) Split it.
JOEY. (*To Butch.*) I'll get it later. We're short handed downstairs. (*He exits.*)
GLADYS. (*Giving her the money.*) The room's paid for, makes it a hundred and a half for you. Not bad, eh?
HELEN. (*Overwhelmed.*) Oh no!

GLADYS. (*Grins at her.*) You're a nice kid. Take it.
HELEN. I couldn't.
GLADYS. I got plenty and Charlie's got more. I want you to have it.
HELEN. (*Finally.*) Well, thank you very much.
BROWN. (*Having been eyeing Helen.*) I'd like to ask you a question.
GLADYS. What is it, Mister Brown?
BROWN. I've paid for this room, haven't I?
GLADYS. Yes.
BROWN. Why don't you all run along and leave this young lady and myself alone? We might have a bite together. (*This is old stuff to Gladys. She nods to Butch, who returns her glance, expressionless. He nods. He steps to Brown, takes him by the scruff of his coat, almost lifting him off the floor, and steers him to the door.*)
BUTCH. We don't allow any biting around here. (*They are out.*)
GLADYS. They get over being nervous real quick. Butch is a real comfort. (*Helen nods, slightly dazed at the events.*)
HELEN. Well, thank you again. I've made two hundred and seventy-five dollars the last half hour!
GLADYS. General Motors should do as well! I'm loaded with their stock!
HELEN. I hope you'll be very happy. I'm sure you will. (*They shake hands, Gladys holds on, an idea forming.*)
GLADYS. Sit down.
HELEN. (*Surprised and puzzled.*) I really have to go—
GLADYS. Sit down! (*Helen does, tentatively.*) I got a superstition. I got it from my old man. He used to say to me, "If you get a lucky break make a lucky break for somebody else." Kind of throw something back into the pot, you know what I mean?
HELEN. (*She nods, but is in the dark.*) Yes.
GLADYS. I like you, I'm going to do something for you. (*Helen waits.*) I'm going to give you a present! My business!
HELEN. Thank you very much, but I really don't—
GLADYS. Now stop beating your gums until I finish talking. You haven't the faintest idea what I'm handing over to you. I don't do this work once in a while, I've got a regular business here.
HELEN. I really wouldn't know how to do it—

GLADYS. You've done it twice, that's how you do it. (*She fiddles in her purse and takes out an appointment book.*) In this book are all the lawyers I deal with. There used to be a lot of tramps doing this, lawyers got into trouble. They trust Bagley. You know, Gladys Bagley isn't really my name. There were five ahead of me. This business has been going on a long time. Keep the firm name, a lot of good will goes with it. (*Indicating the closet.*) You can have my stock of pajamas. You have to keep changing the pajamas or one of the judges'll get suspicious that all the husbands are wearing polka dots. What do you say?

HELEN. (*Sincerely.*) It's very generous of you, really, but the truth is I've just taken a job in Paris.

GLADYS. No kidding? Well, Paris is cute. I been there.

HELEN. I've never looked forward to anything so much in my life.

GLADYS. (*Looking at the appointment book in her hand.*) It's a pity to let the business go to waste. It took a long time to build it up. Know anybody to give it to? Somebody reliable!

HELEN. No, I don't.

GLADYS. I don't either. Oh well, maybe you'll think of someone. Keep the book. (*She throws it on Helen's lap, getting up.*) You wouldn't think a job that clears twenty thousand dollars a year'd go begging.

HELEN. (*Startled.*) Twenty thousand dollars a year!

GLADYS. (*Smiling.*) Net! (*She laughs.*) Honey, you ought to see the look on your face!

HELEN. Twenty thousand dollars!

GLADYS. And it's tax free! (*Beguilingly.*) You can always go to Paris later. It's been there a long time.

HELEN. (*Not strong, thinking.*) No, I have to go now.

GLADYS. Why can't you go a year from now? In style.

HELEN. (*Weaker.*) I have to go now.

GLADYS. Well, it's your life. But I'd think about it if I were you. Opportunity doesn't knock your door down, kid, it only scratches very soft. You've got to listen for it, and when you hear it, you have to grab the door open. Anyway, don't make your mind up now. Sleep on it.

HELEN. (*Unhappily.*) Who'll be able to sleep? (*Gladys laughs loudly at Helen's discomfiture as the lights go out.*)

ACT I

SCENE 5

The lights come up on Barbee's outer office, the next morning. Helen is seated, her hand supporting her chin, wearing the same expression we saw last night. Clearly, she's still thinking about her decision. She shakes her head, sighs.

The buzzer, from Barbee's office, sounds. Helen, lost, is oblivious. It sounds again, more insistent. Helen comes to, with a start, and answers the phone.

HELEN. (*Into phone.*) Yes, Mister Barbee? . . . It must be in the Kelly file, I'll bring it right in. (*She hangs up, goes to the file, opens it and starts to look. Barbee's door opens and he enters.*)
BARBEE. What are you looking for?
HELEN. The Kelly file.
BARBEE. You gave it to me ten minutes ago.
HELEN. I did?
BARBEE. What's the matter with you? Are you all right?
HELEN. I didn't sleep a wink last night. This morning I brushed my teeth with cold cream.
BARBEE. What's bothering you?
HELEN. That job in Paris. I hope I've made the right decision.
BARBEE. Well, you know how I'm voting. I hope you stay here.
HELEN. No, I'm going to take it. But it's a long way to go to get out of riding in a subway.
BARBEE. Are you at least going to find me another secretary?
HELEN. I can interview them first, that'll save you some trouble.
BARBEE. I won't like her. (*The phone rings.*)
HELEN. (*Into phone.*) Edward Barbee, attorney-at-law . . . (*Hand over mouthpiece.*) It's Atlantic City.
BARBEE. MacKelwaine! (*He reaches for the phone.*) Hello? . . . Can't you speak a little louder? (*He puts his hand over the mouthpiece.*) Marilyn is in the bathroom, he doesn't want her to hear him! (*Into mouthpiece.*) I hear you now . . . Listen, you're emotionally upset, don't make any definite promises! Now why don't you come in and talk to me before you do anything! . . . I'll be in all day . . . So long. (*He hangs up.*) He wants to take her to

South America! Would it hurt his divorce? (*He shakes his head.*) I'm going to call up my broker and sell his company short! (*Exiting.*) I'll clean up! (*Helen looks at the phone, shakes her head, and continues typing. The door opens and Woodrow enters.*)
WOODROW. Busy?
HELEN. Well, I may be soon.
WOODROW. I couldn't wait. Did you get the thousand dollars?
HELEN. Uh huh.
WOODROW. What a nice uncle!
HELEN. He's against my going.
WOODROW. But he gave you the money?
HELEN. I was crying—collect.
WOODROW. What's he against?
HELEN. He says I can't live in Paris for sixty dollars a week. He's been there.
WOODROW. He's been at the George Fifth Hotel! As a tourist! We're going to live like natives!
HELEN. How do the natives live?
WOODROW. Fine! You've seen their pictures in the paper! Do they look starved?
HELEN. (*She thinks.*) All I can remember are Brigitte Bardot and Maurice Chevalier. I'm not going to live like them either.
WOODROW. Now look here. There are slight concessions to comfort you make to live in Europe, but they're tiny and superficial. Actually coping with them turns out to be amusing.
HELEN. (*A warning note.*) Let's hear them. I'll tell you whether they're amusing.
WOODROW. Well, would you consider a bathroom down the hall so unbearable?
HELEN. I'm not laughing.
WOODROW. I've got a number of listings of apartments. You can have your choice. There's one in Neuilly that I recommend for you. It's on the top floor, with a view!
HELEN. With an elevator?
WOODROW. It's only five flights! You're young and healthy, the exercise'll give you an appetite!
HELEN. I get hungry without exercise.
WOODROW. And the great thing about this apartment is the subway is right on the corner!
HELEN. (*An involuntary shout.*) The subway!

WOODROW. (*Alarmed.*) What's the matter? What did I say?
HELEN. You said a dirty word! I didn't know Paris even had a subway!
WOODROW. Certainly it has. It's called the Metro. How did you expect to get to work?
HELEN. I don't know! I guess I thought I was going to float in that blue light! (*Sudden determination.*) Forget it! I'm not taking the job!
WOODROW. Why not?
HELEN. Because I don't want to! I woke up this morning with a feeling I was making a mistake! I'm sorry!
WOODROW. Is it the money?
HELEN. Frankly, it is! You're not meeting the competition!
WOODROW. I might go back and get another ten dollars. I had that in mind anyway, but I can't promise.
HELEN. You're still way under the market! Please forget it!
WOODROW. (*Terribly disappointed.*) Well, I can't take that for an answer. I won't.
HELEN. I don't see what alternative you have.
WOODROW. I feel there must be another reason you've changed your mind. Is it something I've said?
HELEN. The word "subway" didn't help.
WOODROW. Yesterday you were so anxious to go. You must have some reason.
HELEN. (*Deciding a white lie is kindest.*) To tell you the truth, my mother won't allow it.
WOODROW. (*He looks at her a moment and she wavers.*) It's been my experience when people start a sentence with "to tell you the truth" it rarely is. I say there's another reason.
HELEN. Are you accusing me of lying?
WOODROW. Possibly.
HELEN. (*Exasperated.*) Would you do me the courtesy of getting out of here? Frankly, the hell out of here?
WOODROW. (*He holds her glance a moment.*) Now I know you're lying. We both know it. (*He turns and strides out. Helen opens her drawer and takes out the perfume bottle.*)
HELEN. (*Banging it on the desk.*) You're forgetting something! (*He slams the door.*) Why, that nervy—the brass—why—! (*She glares at the perfume bottle and drops it in her waste basket. Her purse is in her line of vision, on her desk. She opens it and*

extracts Bagley's telephone book. She riffles through it. She picks up the phone, refers to the book again, and dials.) Hello. May I speak with Mister Duffield? . . . (*She's nervous now.*) This is Miss Bagley. Gladys Bagley . . . Hello, Mister Duffield. I'm fine . . . Well, I'm not that Miss Bagley, I'm the new one . . . She's gotten married . . . I'm sure she'll be happy . . . Yes, I have the same arrangement . . . Well, I'm lucky I called then . . . Next Thursday . . . (*Writing it down.*) Yes, next Thursday is fine. I'll be expecting your client at seven o'clock . . . Not at all, Mister Duffield . . . Thank *you* . . . My number here is Plaza 6-2131, but only for the next two weeks. I'll call again and leave my new number. Good day. (*She hangs up, and exhales softly, relieved.*) That wasn't hard. (*The door opens and Barbee enters, carrying a paper.*)

BARBEE. What's this letter about? I can't read the handwriting.

HELEN. He's a client you divorced three years ago. He'd like a copy of the divorce.

BARBEE. Have we got that here or in storage?

HELEN. I'm not sure. Let me look. (*She gets up to cross to the files, bends down for the bottom one, and the phone rings. Barbee, next to it, picks it up.*)

BARBEE. Hello . . . Who? Bagley? You've got the wrong number—

HELEN. (*Quickly.*) That's for me! (*She takes the phone.*) Yes? . . . Yes I am . . . I understand, Mister Duffield, you can't be too careful. Perfectly all right. Thursday at seven o'clock. (*She hangs up. She is a reluctant liar.*) I gave that name to—someone I didn't want to know my real name.

BARBEE. (*He smiles at her.*) I'm beginning to think you lead a more interesting life than I imagined. Strangers in elevators, fake names on the telephone—. Say, that reminds me. Good you brought up Bagley. Call her.

HELEN. Call her?

BARBEE. Our Mister Cooper is going to get a divorce and needs his picture taken. See if next Monday is all right.

HELEN. (*She makes up her mind.*) What time?

BARBEE. Oh, make it eight o'clock if that's possible.

HELEN. (*Flat.*) Monday at eight'll be fine.

BARBEE. (*Puzzled, he looks to her.*) How do you know?

HELEN. I know.

BARBEE. (*Tinge of sharpness.*) No you don't! We rarely get the appointment we want! Bagley's very busy!
HELEN. I'm Miss Bagley!
BARBEE. (*He hasn't heard as yet.*) We're lucky if we can get— (*It's registered.*) What's that?
HELEN. (*Nodding.*) I'm the new Miss Bagley. She's retired, she gave me her business last night. (*He thinks, looks at the telephone, remembering the recent call, and then at her.*)
BARBEE. Slowly. Say it again.
HELEN. I'm in the Bagley business. Monday night I'll be taking Mister Cooper's picture.
BARBEE. You can't do a thing like that!
HELEN. Why not?
BARBEE. Because you can't!
HELEN. I did it last night. You asked me to.
BARBEE. That was different!
HELEN. What was different about it?
BARBEE. It was an emergency!
HELEN. Mister Barbee, my whole life is an emergency! One big emergency! And do you know what's going to cure it? Money!
BARBEE. What do you need money for?
HELEN. I need money not to ride in the subway during the rush hour. And I need money to look like the women I see on Park Avenue.
BARBEE. You look better than they do!
HELEN. I don't feel it, and that's what counts. They've got confidence. And you know where the confidence comes from? From the French clothes, and the silk underwear, and the shoes and purse that match. (*She shakes her finger at him.*) You take those women eating lunch at the Colony today, you undress them, mix them with a naked group from Klein's Basement, and I tell you the F.B.I. couldn't tell them apart! It's the money that separates the sheep from the goats in this world, and I'm going to be a sheep— (*She's lost now.*) or a goat—or whichever it is that's eating at the Colony! (*They exchange looks for a long moment, we have no indication of Barbee's reaction.*)
BARBEE. (*Finally.*) You may be right. (*He smiles at her.*)
HELEN. (*Fervently, grateful for his approval.*) Thank you, Mister Barbee.
BARBEE. (*Reflectively.*) I sure would like to see those Colony

and Klein's Basement women all naked together. Be damned interesting. (*He starts to his office.*)

HELEN. Are you calling your wife to tell her?

BARBEE. (*At his door.*) Frankly, I'm afraid to. She might want to open a Bagley branch of her own! (*He smiles and closes the door. She takes the appointment book, looks at a number, and dials.*)

HELEN. Hello, may I speak to Mr. Cornish? . . . (*She reaches into the waste basket and retrieves the perfume.*) Miss Bagley . . . Just tell him Miss Bagley—girlie!

(*The curtain starts down.*)

ACT II

SCENE 1

Room 1640.
Three weeks later. Helen has transformed the room with a score of tasteful touches. There are bowls of flowers, a small phonograph with its records in a stand beside it, books, magazines, and on the wall a large travel poster featuring some beauty spot in Europe.
Butch and Joey are playing gin rummy. Butch lays a card down.

JOEY. Why'd you do that for?
BUTCH. I have to give you a reason?
JOEY. You just picked it up!
BUTCH. Now I'm laying it down.
JOEY. You're not fooling me. (*He carefully lays down a card, holding his thumb on it.*)
BUTCH. Ha!
JOEY. (*Pulling the card back.*) Hold it!
BUTCH. (*Protesting.*) Hey!
JOEY. I didn't put it down!
BUTCH. Certainly you did!
JOEY. I had my thumb on it, didn't I? We made a rule, didn't we? If your thumb is still on the card it isn't a laydown! I tricked you! Now I know you want that card! That's called strategy!
BUTCH. I call it crooked!
JOEY. If you understood strategy you'd've been the middleweight champ.
BUTCH. This is the last time we play!
JOEY. (*Throwing out a different card happily.*) Be a sorehead.
BUTCH. (*Taking the card.*) Gin! (*Triumphantly.*) I didn't want the other card! How's that for strategy?
JOEY. I don't want to play anymore.
BUTCH. Oh boy, talk about a sorehead! When you did it—

(*And through the door comes Helen. She is radiant, in an obviously expensive light summer dress. She carries a hat box and other shopping evidence.*)
HELEN. (*In high spirits.*) Hello, boys! (*They leap up in happy anticipation. Helen has evidently two strong admirers.*)
BUTCH AND JOEY. Hi, Helen.
HELEN. What's new?
BUTCH. That dress.
JOEY. (*In admiration.*) Another new one?
HELEN. (*Whirling, modeling.*) Uh huh, how do you like it?
JOEY. I like it because it sticks to you.
BUTCH. Watch your language!
JOEY. What did I say? Did I say anything, Helen?
HELEN. (*Touched by Butch's solicitude.*) That's all right, Butch. He meant it as a compliment, I'm sure. I hope so.
JOEY. Certainly. You got a figure a dress ought to stick to. (*Butch glares at him.*) What's wrong with that?
BUTCH. (*To Helen.*) My wife says to thank you for all the clothes you gave my two girls.
HELEN. Did everything fit?
BUTCH. The younger girl had to have some of the things taken in, but the older one's fit exactly. Even the underwear.
HELEN. (*Putting down her bundles, helped by Joey.*) Good!
BUTCH. Are you sure you didn't make a mistake? My wife says you gave her some things that are like new.
HELEN. I didn't make a mistake. That was all my old wardrobe.
BUTCH. All of it?
HELEN. Uh huh. I've started brand new. Butch, if something nice happens to you, pass it along. Always throw something back into the pot. You know who told me that? Miss Bagley previous.
JOEY. Say, we got another card from her! (*He pulls it out of his pocket.*) From Mexico. (*He reads.*) "Dear Joey and Butch. Look at the fish I caught. It made me sad to catch him but it was his own fault. If he'd kept his mouth shut he wouldn't've gotten in trouble. Miss the hell out of you. Love and kisses. Mrs. Charles Patterson." (*He hands the card to Helen.*) Get the size of that fish!
HELEN. (*Looking at the picture.*) Acapulco! I'm going there one of these days! (*She looks to her poster.*) After Europe! Joey, start the record! (*She gives him the card, going to the phone.*

Butch goes to the chair next to the phonograph, picking up a book which is already open, face down. Into phone.) Hi, Molly! Any calls? . . . Check with my message service, will you? . . . Oh, it was nothing, I thought you'd like it, it's your color . . . You're more than welcome . . . *(She hangs up. The phonograph starts, it's a Teach Yourself French record.)*
PHONOGRAPH. *(Cheerily.)* This is the sixteenth lesson of your Teach Yourself French at Home. How do we say "sixteenth"? Seizieme. Seizieme. Very well, students, let us begin. "Manger," to eat. I eat, you eat, he eats, etcetera. Together!
BUTCH, HELEN AND PHONOGRAPH. *(Together, Helen reciting from memory, Butch reading.)* Je mange, vous mangez, il mange, nous mangeons, ils mangent. *(Helen pronounces the last "Il manj" but Butch says "ill manjon.")*
HELEN. *(To Butch.)* You don't pronounce the last syllable.
PHONOGRAPH. You don't pronounce the last syllable.
HELEN. See?
PHONOGRAPH. We will review our numbers, quickly! Count to ten!
BUTCH, HELEN AND PHONOGRAPH. Un, deux, trois, quatre, cinq, six, sept, huit, neuf, dix.
JOEY. That could come in handy, Butch, in case you get knocked out in France. *(Butch stops the phonograph.)*
BUTCH. *(Elaborate.)* How would you like a frap on the nay, which is French for a punch on the nose!
JOEY. *(Mock.)* Ha ha.
HELEN. Don't tease him, Joey. He's to be admired for trying to learn. I admire you, Butch.
BUTCH. Mairsee bohkoo.
JOEY. Coming outa him it sounds ridiculous. Why is he doing it? You want to be an ambassador or something?
BUTCH. No. *(He smiles mysteriously.)*
HELEN. *(Intrigued.)* Butch, why are you learning French?
BUTCH. My wife and I grew up together on a Hundred and Twenty-Fifth Street. I don't think one thing ever happened to either of us the other doesn't know. One of these days—I don't know where—somebody is going to say something in French around me, and I'm gonna answer him. And Bessie is gonna say—I can hear her saying it—"Butch, why didn't you tell me you

WOODROW. The country's full of crooks! (*Leaning forward, with finger.*) I tell you the moral fibre of this country is being eroded by a total lack of responsibility towards— (*He catches himself and stops.*) Ah, what the hell, this isn't the place for it! Anyway, I'm being sent to Paris. I need an American legal secretary, the job only pays sixty dollars! What do I do? Call up the President and ask him to raise your salary?
HELEN. I wouldn't think so.
WOODROW. After we had our door slamming scene I put your name in for a Civil Service classification that does pay a hundred dollars a week and I thought my boss was going to hit me with a lamp! He said I was robbing the American people. My boss thinks he's Nathan Hale.
HELEN. You put my name in for a government job?
WOODROW. You didn't have to take it, it didn't obligate you in any way. It was just one of my desperate moves. (*There is a moment of silence.*) Will you have dinner with me?
HELEN. (*Stalling.*) I don't believe I can. I have to work. I'm expecting a client.
WOODROW. (*He sits.*) I'll wait.
HELEN. (*She gets up.*) You never know how long the work'll be. I'm eating here, I was ordering when you came in.
WOODROW. (*A moment.*) Can I see you after you've finished your work? No matter what time it is.
HELEN. It isn't just the dictation, I have to transcribe the notes. Sometimes I'm not through until quite late— (*And through the door comes Gladys, tanned, dressed to the hilt, in her usual exuberance.*)
GLADYS. (*Loud.*) Watch the birdie! Hi ya, kid! (*Woodrow stands up.*)
HELEN. (*Going to her, apprehensive.*) Mrs. Patterson, what a surprise! I thought you were in Mexico! A postal came from you only today!
GLADYS. We made up our minds suddenly and flew in! You look great!
HELEN. So do you! You're so tan! How did you like Mexico?
GLADYS. (*A grin.*) It's full of Mexicans! I'm crazy about dark men and they're crazy about blondes, we got along fine!
HELEN. (*Obliged.*) May I introduce Mrs. Gladys Patterson. Mister Woodrow O'Malley.

WOODROW. How do you do.
GLADYS. How do you do.
HELEN. (*Pointedly.*) Mrs. Patterson had this public stenographer's office before me.
GLADYS. (*Getting it.*) Uh huh.
HELEN. In fact, she gave me her business because she was getting married.
GLADYS. What's the use of being married if you have to keep typing?
HELEN. I'd like to have dinner with you, but we've got a lot to talk about, and a client's coming—
GLADYS. (*Thinking she's helping.*) Hold it! You want to have dinner with him? Run along! We can chew the rag any time, I'll take care of the client!
HELEN. No, it's really not necessary, I don't want to put you to all that trouble—
GLADYS. (*Taking her jacket off.*) Forget it! Charlie went to his club to see the boys, and I want to visit with Butch and Joey. I thought I'd have to go to a movie! Go on, beat it, have a good time! What's the matter, you afraid I've forgoten how to type?
HELEN. (*Smiles.*) No.
GLADYS. What's the name of the client?
HELEN. Mister Knudsen.
GLADYS. Knudsen. Take care of him fine.
WOODROW. I'm much obliged, Mrs. Patterson.
GLADYS. My pleasure.
HELEN. (*To Woodrow.*) I don't have to go home to change, I have a dress here.
WOODROW. Great. I'll be in the bar. I'm happy to have met you, Mrs. Patterson. *Very* happy.
GLADYS. Likewise. (*He's out.*) Cute kid.
HELEN. Not that cute. He works for the Income Tax Department.
GLADYS. (*Easily.*) No kidding?
HELEN. Can you imagine? Of all the jobs in the world! I don't need him hanging around here! Luckily, he's going to Paris next week and I'm rid of him! (*She starts to the closet, and will change into a black dress during the scene.*) Tell me about Mexico, and married life!

GLADYS. Well, they're both very nice, but you got to get used to them.
HELEN. Charlie still give you that big charge?
GLADYS. Yeah. (*New tone.*) He gives it to me. (*Far away voice.*) The trouble is I don't give it to him. (*Helen looks at her sharply. For a moment Gladys fights it and then she quickly opens her purse and takes out her handkerchief into which she starts to cry. Helen comes to her. Gladys' body is shaken with sobs.*)
HELEN. I'm sorry. (*She recovers, blowing.*)
GLADYS. Excuse me.
HELEN. That's all right.
GLADYS. I don't like people who share their troubles.
HELEN. You have to let it out someplace.
GLADYS. (*After a moment.*) I've had it bottled up so long I think my head's going to explode.
HELEN. Maybe things aren't as bad as you imagine.
GLADYS. Yes, they are.
HELEN. People quarrel in the beginning—
GLADYS. We've never had a quarrel. (*Flat.*) I came in from the beach to get a sweater, and I was in the closet, and he came in to take a long distance call. I stayed in the closet. I wasn't trying to eavesdrop, I was going to come out of the closet naked. It was still our honeymoon. And I heard the telephone call.
HELEN. I see.
GLADYS. He's got a sweetheart. It's the one he left his wife for. But he hasn't any money. (*Slowly.*) And he's going to—"milk the stupid old bag"— (*Deliberately.*) —that's what he called me, "the stupid old bag." I didn't come out of the closet. When he left I went to the bathroom—I'm not sure but I think I was considering killing myself—hard to believe, isn't it?—but then I remembered if I killed myself he'd get my money.
HELEN. Have you told him you know?
GLADYS. Not yet. I'm going to pack first. Then I'm going to tell him. I've got a hell of a speech prepared.
HELEN. Is there anything I can do?
GLADYS. (*She shakes her head.*) I'm moving to this hotel, I don't know anyone at the Astor. I don't want the business back, if that's what you're thinking.
HELEN. You're entitled to it.
GLADYS. Keep it. I just need people to talk to. Butch and Joey

are about all I got. (*She is fighting crying again and Helen puts her arm around her.*)
HELEN. Now you perk up. We're going to have a lot of fun together, you see if we don't (*She resumes her dressing.*) Take care of Mister Knudsen, go to the Astor and pack your things, make your speech to Charlie boy, and move in here! Tonight we go to a midnight movie!
GLADYS. What about your date? I don't want to start spoiling things.
HELEN. The income tax man? I'm going to get rid of *him* as soon as I can, he's nobody I want to know! (*She's about to leave.*)
GLADYS. (*Emotionally.*) I can't tell you how grateful I am.
HELEN. (*At the door.*) An old friend taught me a wonderful saying, "Always put something back in the pot." (*A wave and she's out. The lights go down.*)

ACT II

SCENE 2

The lights come up on Helen and Woodrow in the same restaurant we have seen earlier.
They seat themselves.

WOODROW. Are you sure this restaurant suits you?
HELEN. I liked the food last time. I'm going to order chicken in the pot again. Pot au feu! It tastes better in French. (*Our old waiter enters, gives them menus.*)
WAITER. Buon giorno.
WOODROW. Buon giorno? What happened to "Bonjour"?
WAITER. This is an Italian restaurant now! (*Recognizing them.*) Hey, how are you?
HELEN. Fine.
WAITER. I remember you two. Chicken in the pot. Some memory, eh?
WOODROW. Why are you an Italian restaurant?
WAITER. Why do you think why? We were starving to death! We were eating the chickens in the pot. So my smart brother-in-law thinks an Italian restaurant'll go better. Now I say "Buon giorno."

HELEN. Are you doing better?
WAITER. Just the same. Nothing helps. My brother-in-law's thinking of changing it to a Chinese restaurant. Wait till you hear me say "Hello" in Chinese. Well, what'll it be?
HELEN. I was looking forward to chicken in the pot. I guess you haven't got it now.
WAITER. Certainly! It's the same menu with spaghetti!
HELEN. Good, that's what I'll have.
WOODROW. I will, too.
WAITER. Keep coming back, I promise you it'll be here when we're a Chinese restaurant! (*He goes.*)
WOODROW. They're enterprising, anyway. (*He looks at her, happily. She must say something.*)
HELEN. I'm curious about something. If you're in the income tax department why are you going abroad?
WOODROW. American companies have branches abroad. They cheat too.
HELEN. That's not a nice word.
WOODROW. No. The right word is "steal." If you cheat on your income tax you're stealing. You're stealing from your government and your fellow citizens. (*Evidently her expression has reflected something.*) I use "you" in the figurative sense.
HELEN. Thank you.
WOODROW. If the right word was used more there might be less of it. I regret to inform you a large number of the great American public are dishonest. It's a puzzle to me that the same citizen who'll die for his countdy won't file an honest tax return.
HELEN. You're very cynical.
WOODROW. My experience would sour a saint. One man listed his cat as a dependent. Another prominent citizen didn't know his father and mother had died two years before, they were still listed as deductions. We found out he'd been to the funerals. I'm happy to say he's in jail.
HELEN. You're gloating about it. You like your job.
WOODROW. I'm not gloating, but I like my job. I like working for the United States government, and so does my father, who's a letter carrier, I'm proud to be an income tax man, and I'm going to be prouder, when I'm older and have proven I deserve it, to be head of the Bureau. Which is why I offer you a thousand dollars of my own savings, which are not very large, because the

job in Paris badly needs someone who understands American contracts. I'm not being especially patriotic, I want to make a record for myself. Will you take the job?
HELEN. It isn't convenient right now. (*She searches his face.*) You haven't much of a sense of humour about your job.
WOODROW. I've been told I haven't. I restrain myself from spitting in the eye of a brother citizen about twice a day. Usually when I'm being bribed. I used to bring charges against them, but my boss—the one who's ordinarily Nathan Hale—is more charitable. He doesn't let me press the charge. I consider a man who will bribe a public official contemptible and criminal, and when I am head of the Internal Revenue Service I will throw each and every one into the clink.
HELEN. It'll have to be a pretty big clink. You're an angry young man.
WOODROW. Not at all. I'm witty and charming and in many ways stupid, I've been sorry to discover, but I'm not angry at the world, or the older generation, or anything else. I'm happy to be alive, and if the world'll let me stay alive, I'll be very grateful and contribute what I can to order and decency, including three or four children reared with respect for church, family and fellow man.
HELEN. Do you often talk like this?
WOODROW. How am I talking?
HELEN. Kind of sing song. Like a drunk.
WOODROW. I had a drink. I couldn't sit in the bar of your hotel without ordering one. However, I don't believe I'm intoxicated, merely happy. (*A moment.*) I don't recall any reaction from you to my expectation of three or four children. What do you think of the number?
HELEN. On a government salary?
WOODROW. We have five in my family.
HELEN. (*Not seriously.*) Show me a picture of your mother.
WOODROW. Very well. (*He extracts a wallet.*)
HELEN. I was teasing.
WOODROW. (*Showing.*) Here you are. (*Pointing.*) Mother, father, oldest, next oldest, next oldest, me, the youngest. That's a dog.
HELEN. (*Sincerely.*) You're a fine looking family.
WOODROW. My mother doesn't seem haggard.

HELEN. (*For amusement.*) You might have retouched it. I'd like to speak to her.
WOODROW. Couldn't be easier to arrange. Sunday dinner at my house. What my mother can do is cook!
HELEN. (*Thrown.*) I couldn't do that—
WOODROW. She asked you.
HELEN. She did? How does she know me?
WOODROW. I speak to her.
HELEN. I really couldn't. I—I have to see my own family Sunday night.
WOODROW. Sunday lunch would be all right.
HELEN. It wouldn't be quite convenient. Let it go this week.
WOODROW. I'm leaving in four days.
HELEN. (*A simulated enthusiasm.*) I tell you what. Let's make a date for Paris. Right now. One year from tonight! What do you say? We'll do the town, and it'll be my treat!
WOODROW. The government doesn't pay me that little.
HELEN. I didn't mean it that way. I'd be grateful for someone to show me around. (*There is a silence, Woodrow quite disappointed. Into the scene, from* L., *evidently passing from one section of the restaurant to another, comes Turner. He has had one drink too many and is slightly louder than normal.*)
TURNER. (*Delighted.*) Hey! Hi! What a surprise! (*No reaction from frozen Helen.*) Don't you remember me with my clothes on?
HELEN. I beg your pardon.
TURNER. (*Only meaning to be funny.*) We were in bed together!
HELEN. You must be mistaken! (*Woodrow stands up, mad.*)
WOODROW. Get the hell out of here! (*Turner looks to him and then to Helen. Now he gets it.*)
TURNER. I'm terribly sorry. I thought you were someone else.
WOODROW. (*Quieter.*) Just run along.
TURNER. I guess I've had a drink too many. (*To Helen.*) Excuse me.
WOODROW. Okay. (*He goes off,* R. *Woodrow sits.*) Don't let it upset you.
HELEN. I'm not upset. (*There is a pause. Woodrow is debating with himself.*)
WOODROW. (*Finally.*) Helen. (*She looks to him.*) It's the first time I've called you that. Out loud. Helen. (*Solemnly.*) I'm going to ask you to marry me. Would you please marry me?

HELEN. (*Disturbed.*) You're flattering, but not realistic.
WOODROW. I'm being very realistic, I only have four days. I love you. I've never asked anyone to marry me before.
HELEN. (*Uncomfortable.*) We don't know each other.
WOODROW. Give me the next four days. Come see my family. Let me do what I can to sell myself.
HELEN. (*Touched by his sincerity.*) Marriage is for a lifetime. Or should be. Being compatible in a restaurant isn't enough. (*He says nothing, which is unnerving.*) This crush you have on me—or whatever it is—is only in your imagination.
WOODROW. Where else would it be? Love has to be in the imagination. You're only a few dollars worth of chemicals and about sixty percent water, if I remember my high school science. I thought about that during the sleeping pills. I tried picturing you as a jar full of calcium and a bathtub full of water. It didn't help. (*Helen meets his solemn gaze as long as she can.*)
HELEN. Let's wait until Paris.
WOODROW. It's a year. (*They sit in silence. The waiter enters with the soup bowls on a tray.*)
WAITER. (*Placing the bowl before Helen.*) I put aside two prune whips. They're the last ones. If you don't want them tell me. My advice is take them— (*In placing the bowl before Woodrow it slips, and a considerable amount is spilled on his coat.*) Oooops! I'm sorry! (*Woodrow has jumped up.*) You get burned?
WOODROW. (*Altogether unhappy.*) No, no.
WAITER. (*Inspecting the large, visible stain.*) We have to get that spot out!
WOODROW. It's all right. Don't worry about it.
WAITER. Listen, that's real chicken soup! You can get it out now, you can't get it out tomorrow. (*He lifts him by the arm.*) The men's room attendant'll fix it. He knows how. Go on! (*Since he is being pulled, Woodrow decides to go.*)
WOODROW. Excuse me. (*He leaves,* R.)
WAITER. (*Adjusting the damage on the table.*) The coat'll be all right. I've spilled a lot of chicken soup in my life. You know what's the hardest thing to get out? You'll never guess. Tomato sauce! Why is that? The men's room attendant can't do a thing with it. I try not to spill tomato sauce anymore. (*From* L. *comes a thirty year old policeman, John. He walks directly to* R., *exiting.*)
HELEN. (*Having watched his progress.*) Is anything the matter?

WAITER. No, he's the cop on this beat. We give him the courtesy of the men's room. That boy friend of yours has a very nice character. Ask me how I know?
HELEN. (*Smile.*) How do you know?
WAITER. You can always tell a man's character how be behaves when you spill something on him.
HELEN. People behave differently?
WAITER. Ho ho! From wanting to give you a punch on the nose to telling you please not to worry. You notice your boy friend said for me not to worry. (*A wink.*) Grab him, that's the kind of husband to have.
HELEN. I can spill chicken soup on him all day! (*The waiter laughs, delighted, and there is a sudden loud noise from* R., *punctuated with unidentifiable shouts. Both look* R.)
WAITER. Hey, what's that? Excuse me. (*He hurries* R. *Helen, concerned, looks in that direction, halting eating. The men's voices continue, and now Turner and Woodrow appear, accompanied by policeman John. The waiter trails after them. Turner has a handkerchief to a bleeding nose.*)
WOODROW. (*As he reaches Helen.*) Please call Plaza 9-7501 and tell the man who answers to come to the 47th Street Police Station. Plaza 9-7501. (*The waiter writes it on his pad as the trio exit* L.)
WAITER. I have it. (*Helen turns from Woodrow to the waiter and back to the exiting Woodrow, bewildered. The waiter tears the page off his notebook and puts it on the table.*)
HELEN. What happened?
WAITER. Your feller didn't like something that man said to his friend. The attendant said he didn't hear it exactly but it was something about the Mansvoort Hotel. Your boy friend turned him around and hit him. Just with his left hand. He's not a prize fighter, is he?
HELEN. No, he isn't.
WAITER. Well, he's got a hell of a left hand. He knocked the guy over the sink and into the mirror. It's cracked. The bad part is the policeman being a witness, makes it very hard to beat.
HELEN. (*Getting up.*) He needs a lawyer! (*She takes the paper from the table, looking at it.*) Where's the phone, please?
WAITER. Go in the office and phone. I'll bring your soup. (*She exits quickly. He carries the soup. He looks at it.*) Is it cold? (*He*

takes a spoonful and tastes it.) It's fine. *(He continues. Lights out.)*

ACT II

SCENE 3

The lights come up on the 47th Street Police Station. A large and competent Sergeant is behind the raised desk, answering the phone. R., *an open door, leading to some room from which a televised prize fight is heard.* L., *a closed door, leading to the detention rooms. On a wooden bench, facing front, are Helen and Turner. Turner puts a wet handkerchief to his nose once in a while.*

SERGEANT. *(Into phone, writing on his pad.)* Don't be excited, madam, talk slower . . . Five feet nine, glasses, brown suit, mole on his chin . . . If he had an accident, then the hospital'd call you, madam . . . Well, we don't send out bulletins, that'd be the Bureau of Missing Persons . . . Excuse me, madam, how long you been married? . . . A week. I think it's a little early to send out a search party, ma'am, why don't you wait a few hours, he may be playing pool or been caught in a traffic jam or something . . . He doesn't play pool . . . Well, we've had a lot of traffic jams . . . I wouldn't worry, ma'am . . . You're welcome, that's what we're here for. *(He hangs up. Placid.)* That's what we're here for. *(There is an excited roar from the television broadcast. The Sergeant looks to it. The announcer can be heard counting. The Sergeant shouts.)* Who's down? *(The announcer is heard. "He's up!!" The Sergeant leaves the desk and hurries out,* R.*)*
HELEN. *(Tentatively.)* Your nose is bleeding again, Mister Turner. *(Turner glares at her.)* Shall I get you another piece of ice? *(He ignores her.)* Keep your head back, Mister Turner. *(From* D. L. *comes Barbee. Helen jumps up.)* Oh, Mister Barbee! Thank you for coming!
BARBEE. Start from the beginning.
TURNER. I didn't expect your divorce services to include being punched on the nose!

HELEN. It was a misunderstanding, Mister Turner. (*To Barbee.*) Please tell him to drop the charges!
TURNER. The hell I will!
BARBEE. You'll have to start earlier than that.
TURNER. I was in the men's room of a restaurant and her boy friend knocked me down!
HELEN. You shouldn't have said we were in bed together, Mister Turner.
TURNER. We were, weren't we?
HELEN. But you know the impression you gave—
BARBEE. Hold it! Hold it! Where's the defendant?
HELEN. (*Indicating* L.) He's in there. Locked up. Mister Turner, he has a job with the government, this could be very bad for him.
TURNER. I hope so!
BARBEE. Now look here, Turner, let's consider this—
TURNER. Are you my lawyer or his lawyer?
BARBEE. I'm your lawyer.
TURNER. I want to prefer charges against him! Prefer 'em! Represent me!
BARBEE. Well, you're within your rights—
TURNER. You're damned right I am!
BARBEE. (*Carefully.*) Of course we'll have to stop your divorce proceedings.
TURNER. What's that? Why?
BARBEE. Well, we'll be obliged to explain how you know this young lady. And what you meant when you said you were in bed together.
TURNER. I don't see how that'll come up!
BARBEE. I don't see how it'll be avoided. (*The Sergeant returns from* R.) How do you do, Sergeant?
SERGEANT. You the young's man's lawyer?
TURNER. He's *my* lawyer!
SERGEANT. (*Puzzled, to Helen.*) Isn't this the lawyer you're waiting for?
HELEN. (*Rattled.*) He's both their lawyers. I mean, he's the lawyer for both of them.
SERGEANT. (*Looking from one to the other. Pointing off,* L.) He hit him, and you called a lawyer, and this lawyer is also *his* lawyer?
HELEN. Yes.

SERGEANT. (*He thinks a moment. All wait.*) Did you know this man before the fight in the men's room?
HELEN. (*Hesitantly.*) Yes.
SERGEANT. How? (*Barbee looks significantly to Turner.*)
TURNER. (*A moment.*) Sergeant, on reflection I don't think I'd care to press charges.
SERGEANT. You don't? Half an hour ago you wanted to send him to jail for life.
TURNER. My nose was bleeding then, Sergeant. I'd like to be generous.
SERGEANT. Well, it's your nose. (*Exiting* L.) Bring him right out. (*Helen waits until he's gone.*)
HELEN. Thank you, Mister Turner. I appreciate it.
TURNER. Your boy friend better appreciate it.
HELEN. You won't say how you know me? The bed part?
BARBEE. I wouldn't. In front of the Sergeant.
TURNER. I'll accept his apology. (*The Sergeant returns, Woodrow behind him.*)
SERGEANT. This man is willing to drop the assault and battery charge.
BARBEE. Very generously.
HELEN. You ought to thank him, Woodrow.
BARBEE. And apologize.
WOODROW. Thank him? Apologize? Certainly not!
TURNER. You won't?
WOODROW. I'm thinking of knocking you down again!
SERGEANT. I wouldn't do that.
BARBEE. The second time gets very complicated. Judges don't like it.
SERGEANT. Listen to your lawyer.
WOODROW. (*To Turner.*) You foul mouthed liar. I'd like nothing better than to explain it to a judge, and a jury, if possible. (*There is a moment.*)
SERGEANT. (*To Turner.*) Your move. Do I book him? (*Turner, at a loss, looks to Barbee. Barbee takes him under the arm.*)
BARBEE. Mister Turner waives the apology. Good night all.
TURNER. (*Being dragged, over his shoulder.*) You're lucky I feel generous, young man!
WOODROW. (*After him.*) You're lucky you're in a police station! (*Barbee and Turner are out,* L.)

HELEN. We can go now. (*The telephone rings, the Sergeant goes to it.*)
SERGEANT. No, you can't. The arresting officer is the complaining witness, he has to drop *his* charge. Stay here! (*Into phone.*) Forty seventh street . . . yes madam . . . your husband's back . . . Very well, we won't send out a search party. He *was* shooting pool . . . No trouble at all, mam. (*He hangs up.*) You wait till the officer comes back, he's on a call. (*The fight broadcast attracts him.*) Just sit down. (*He exits* R. *They sit.*)
HELEN. (*She observes him a moment.*) You all right?
WOODROW. Of course!
HELEN. You're odd, you know that?
WOODROW. Why?
HELEN. I thought the knight in armor type'd died out.
WOODROW. Knight in armor type? Because I knocked down a stupid drunk?
HELEN. Well, other things, too. Your attitude about your job and all.
WOODROW. (*A lecture again.*) That drunk is a point I was making about public morality. Simple decency— (*He stops abruptly.*)
HELEN. What's the matter?
WOODROW. I was starting a lecture again. I've been told it's a failing of mine. Change the subject.
HELEN. What do you want to talk about?
WOODROW. The last subject of interest was my asking you to marry me.
HELEN. I'm going to see you in Paris next year. But we can write each other.
WOODROW. I'm not much of a letter writer. And the letters I'd like to write shouldn't be dictated. Not even to a French secretary. (*From* L. *enters Harold Haskell. He is sixty, paternal, shrewd. Woodrow rises.*) Hello, Mister Haskell. May I present Miss Helen Foster, Mister Harold Haskell.
HELEN. How do you do.
HASKELL. How do you do. We met on the telephone. She asked me to come here. What trouble are you in?
WOODROW. I knocked someone down.
HELEN. In front of a policeman. Protecting my good name. But

the—knockee—withdrew the charge. Now the policeman has to agree.

HASKELL. Knockee?

WOODROW. She's the legal secretary I told you about. (*Haskell looks intently at Helen.*) You remember our talk about Miss Foster?

HASKELL. I don't see how I could forget it. Your contention was if we didn't employ this young lady the government would topple.

WOODROW. I'm sorry you had to come here.

HASKELL. That's all right. You got me out of a bad bridge game. (*The Sergeant comes back.*)

SERGEANT. (*To the newcomer, with a tinge of sarcasm.*) Another lawyer?

HASKELL. No, I'm not a lawyer. (*Gives it to him.*) My card, Sergeant.

SERGEANT. (*Reading confidently.*) Mister Harold Haskell—Bureau of— (*The confidence oozes out.*) Internal Revenue. (*A pause. Respectfully.*) Are you here to see me?

HASKELL. (*Looking at him, simply.*) Would there be any reason for my seeing you?

SERGEANT. I explained about that contribution to the Police Fund! It never came to me! I handed it right over! I know it looked funny because it was in cash, but I can prove—

HASKELL. (*To relieve his suffering.*) I'm not here to see you, Sergeant. I'm here on behalf of this young man.

SERGEANT. Oh. Well, the charge's been withdrawn— (*Officer John enters.*) Here's the complaining officer! (*Firmly.*) John, that fellow who was knocked down's dropped his charge!

JOHN. He has? (*He looks at Woodrow.*) Well, I saw him knock him down, I'll sign the complaint.

SERGEANT. (*Meaningly.*) Mister Haskell is in the Income Tax Bureau. (*Toward Woodrow.*) And I imagine he is?

HASKELL. He is.

SERGEANT. That's what I thought. (*He looks to John.*)

JOHN. (*He understands.*) Well, if the man who was hit's withdrawn the charge that's enough for me. He might have slipped.

SERGEANT. There you are!

WOODROW. Not at all! He didn't slip, I hit him! To my discredit, you don't hit drunks! You do your duty, officer. You book

me and I'll take my chances with a judge. (*The Sergeant looks to Haskell.*)
HASKELL. (*Firm.*) The officer is not sure the man didn't slip!
JOHN. No, I'm not.
WOODROW. But I'm sure!
HASKELL. Well, it's your word against his! They say you're released!
SERGEANT. (*Quickly.*) That's right! John, type out the report and he'll sign it. (*To Woodrow.*) Only take a minute. (*Woodrow gives in with bad grace, John starts to the door,* R., *and stops.*)
JOHN. About that husband beating his wife at the Astor. He was gone when I got there. She was beaten up pretty bad, but she wouldn't prefer charges. She checked out.
SERGEANT. Okay. What was that name again?
JOHN. Patterson. Mr. and Mrs. Charles Patterson.
SERGEANT. Patterson. Okay. (*Helen stands up on the announcement of the name. The Sergeant looks to the men.*) You gentlemen interested in the Nelson-Petrelli fight? It's pretty good.
HASKELL. No, thanks.
SERGEANT. (*Going* R.) Be back in a minute. (*He's out.*)
HELEN. I'm afraid I have to leave right now. I—just remembered I have a client.
WOODROW. Won't I see you this evening?
HELEN. Well, if you like, I can see you later.
WOODROW. I'll come to the hotel.
HELEN. (*Quickly.*) No! (*Improvising.*) Clients don't like it. They dictate personal business. Meet me in the lobby in an hour.
WOODROW. Okay.
HELEN. Nice to have met you, Mister Haskell.
HASKELL. Likewise. (*She's out. Haskell looks from her to Woodrow.*) Woodrow!
WOODROW. Yes sir.
HASKELL. I'm reasonably fond of you.
WOODROW. Thank you.
HASKELL. I don't know if I've shown it, I've made an effort to conceal it as a matter of office policy, but the proof of what I think of you is your appointment to the Paris office. A good deal ahead of your seniority.
WOODROW. Yes sir.
HASKELL. I have no complaint against you as a worker,

WOODROW. But you have some other complaint?
HASKELL. (*Simply.*) Yes I have. To put it bluntly, your sense of ethics is a pain in the behind.
WOODROW. I'm sorry.
HASKELL. Don't you ever see anything but black or white?
WOODROW. Something is either ethical or it isn't.
HASKELL. Not at all. Between black and white is gray!
WOODROW. (*Courteously.*) But if it doesn't seem gray to me, sir? If it's recognizably black?
HASKELL. (*He shakes his head, smiles wryly.*) You'll soften as you get older, I hope. Meanwhile I pity the American taxpayer in Paris.
WOODROW. The dishonest taxpayer.
HASKELL. (*Eyes him a moment and gets up.*) Back to my bridge game.
WOODROW. May I take a minute of your time on business, sir?
HASKELL. Certainly.
WOODROW. I'd like to ask you again to let me have a legal secretary at a hundred dollars a week.
HASKELL. Didn't you tell me this young lady wasn't interested in the job?
WOODROW. She's not. I'd like to look for another competent girl, but I have to offer the prevailing wage.
HASKELL. You're not still trying to talk that girl into it?
WOODROW. I tried and I failed. Now I'm trying to talk her into marrying me, and I'm failing there, too. When she comes to Paris next year I'll try again.
HASKELL. (*He looks at him a long moment, debating with himself. He sits.*) I've explained I'm fond of you, how fond are you of me? Outside your job.
WOODROW. I admire you a great deal, Mister Haskell. I believe you know that.
HASKELL. (*Still hesitating.*) I'm taking an awful risk—
WOODROW. What is it, sir?
HASKELL. Do you remember the day you asked me for a hundred dollar secretary and I threw a fit?
WOODROW. Very well.
HASKELL. When you left the office I decided you needed one. And to get around the Table of Organization I put Miss Helen Foster's name in for a Civil Service rating.

WOODROW. (*Encouraging him to continue.*) Yes sir?
HASKELL. (*Flat.*) This involves a security check.
WOODROW. She certainly passed the security check?
HASKELL. Well, she's not a spy, if that's what you think I'm implying.
WOODROW. I don't know what you're implying. What is she?
HASKELL. (*Quietly, evenly.*) She's a call girl.
WOODROW. (*After a moment.*) I knocked a man down for implying that today.
HASKELL. I wouldn't like you to knock me down.
WOODROW. I know she's a legal secretary who was working for a lawyer named Barbee.
HASKELL. That's what she was. Now she's a Public Stenographer at the Mansvoort Hotel, which has another Public Stenographer in the lobby. A real one. You won't find a sheet of carbon paper in her room, but you will find an assortment of men's pajamas. It was quite a thorough security check. Her client at the hotel may be waiting to give her dictation, nine o'clock at night, but I doubt it. (*Woodrow thinks back to what he knows.*) I wouldn't have mentioned it if you hadn't mentioned "marriage." (*John comes out of the room,* R., *with a sheet of paper on a pad, and a pen.*)
JOHN. Just sign here, on the bottom, and everything's okay! (*Woodrow looks at the paper, hardly seeing it.*)
HASKELL. (*Gently.*) Sign it. (*Woodrow does. Haskell looks at him. The Sergeant exits.*) Come on, I'll buy you a drink. (*For a moment, Woodrow still stares, and then he abruptly stands up and strides out. The lights go down.*)

ACT II

SCENE 4

The lights come up on Mansvoort Hotel Room.
Butch and Joey are attending Gladys who is leaning back in a chair, having her eye attended to by Butch. Joey holds a basin of water, Butch has a towel and a small bottle of coagulant.

GLADYS. Ow!
BUTCH. (*In repressed anger.*) Try and hold still.
GLADYS. It hurts.
BUTCH. It's almost over.
JOEY. If he hit her with his fist why would her face be cut like that?
BUTCH. (*Working.*) He was wearing a ring.
GLADYS. Yes he was. I gave it to him. (*Butch works further and is finished. When he steps back we see Gladys has an enormous black eye and cut cheek.*)
BUTCH. You'll have a scar on your cheek but a doctor can take it off. (*Gladys lifts the purse mirror she has in her hand and looks at herself.*)
GLADYS. (*Flat, bitter.*) What difference'll it make?
BUTCH. Your eye'll go down in two days.
GLADYS. (*Looking at it in mirror.*) I don't think it'll go down in a month!
BUTCH. Two days!
JOEY. He knows about black eyes! (*Butch looks at him, still in his tight-lipped mood. Joey is sincere.*) I didn't mean it funny!
BUTCH. (*Deceptively simple.*) Where is your—husband?
GLADYS. (*Looks at him, a moment.*) Why do you want to know?
BUTCH. No reason. Just curious.
JOEY. (*Watching Butch's face, concerned.*) Don't tell him, Gladys! (*Butch looks to him.*) He wants to hit him! He'll get in trouble!
BUTCH. Why don't you mind your own business.
JOEY. He's not allowed to hit anyone, Gladys! They'll throw him in the can!
GLADYS. Forget it, Butch. (*She smiles at him.*) Ow! Smiling's out! (*She looks into the mirror again.*) That shouldn't be a problem. I don't know where he is, Butch, and that's the way I want to leave it.
JOEY. Are you gonna have to stay married to him?
GLADYS. Know any way I can get out of it?
BUTCH. Yeah. Tell me where he is. (*Gladys looks at him fondly.*)
JOEY. Don't do it, Gladys.
GLADYS. Thanks anyway, Butch. (*The door opens, admitting Helen in a hurry. She looks to Gladys.*)

HELEN. Oh, my God! (*She comes to her, discarding her purse.*)
GLADYS. I thought I didn't like my looks before, now I wish I had 'em back.
BUTCH. You're going to look the same!
GLADYS. (*An attempt to amuse the horrified Helen.*) Wasn't worth the trouble then, was it?
HELEN. What a horrible, horrible man!
GLADYS. You're close.
JOEY. He hit her with a fist, with a ring on, and he kicked her.
GLADYS. Missed me a couple of times. I lost the decision though. I was robbed.
HELEN. (*Impressed.*) How can you behave like this?
GLADYS. (*Dropping the assumed banter tone.*) How do you want me to behave?
HELEN. Don't you want to lie down?
GLADYS. I was down. I like being up better. (*She looks at her watch.*) Mister Knudsen'll be here in a couple of minutes.
HELEN. Hasn't he been here?
GLADYS. He called up and changed it to ten o'clock. That's how I had time to go to the Astor and make my speech to Charlie boy.
HELEN. Did you get to make it?
GLADYS. All but the punch line. He beat me to it. That's not bad. (*She smiles, and winces.*) Ow! (*To Butch and Joey.*) Get ready for Mister Knudsen.
HELEN. Forget Mister Knudsen. He can come back tomorrow.
GLADYS. No, you mustn't do that. You've got a business. Keep the store open. Go on, boys. Order some beers for us in my room. I'm moved in next door. (*The two men start out, Gladys and Helen watching them. The door closes behind them.*)
HELEN. Was it terrible?
GLADYS. I didn't like it. But you want to know something? If I had my choice—no speech or no beating—I'd still take the beating. It was a hell of a speech.
HELEN. What did he say?
GLADYS. I didn't leave any pauses where he could get in. When I came to, he was gone. And do you know what he'd done?
HELEN. What?
GLADYS. He'd gone through my purse! Thirty lousy bucks!
HELEN. Is there any chance he'd look for you again?
GLADYS. He's afraid I'm looking for him! Take my word for it,

he's thirty dollars away from here by now. (*The door opens and Woodrow stands there. He was not sure what he would see, and his expression and stance are rigid. Helen is surprised, Gladys is at ease.*) Come on in! (*The sight of Gladys' appearance has upset Woodrow's singleness of purpose. He looks at her while he closes the door.*)

HELEN. I asked you to wait for me in the lobby.

GLADYS. You may not remember me but we met this afternoon. I'm very changeable.

WOODROW. I remember you.

GLADYS. I ran into a bus in my bedroom. Well, I'll leave you two alone. Although that's how the trouble always starts. (*To Helen, as she goes.*) If you need help, you know where I am. I promise I won't come! (*She's out.*)

HELEN. She's had an accident.

WOODROW. I imagine. Hazards of the profession. (*Helen is slightly puzzled at this remark but is occupied with other thoughts.*)

HELEN. (*Looking at her watch.*) I'm expecting my client. I wouldn't like you to be here when he comes.

WOODROW. I'm sure you wouldn't.

HELEN. (*Uncomfortable.*) Staring isn't very courteous.

WOODROW. It isn't very helpful either. I was counting you'd turn into calcium and water, but you haven't yet.

HELEN. I haven't the faintest idea what you're talking about. (*He doesn't move.*) I wish you'd go down to the lobby. Or home if you feel like it.

WOODROW. (*Still searching her face.*) It's remarkable. You'd fool anyone.

HELEN. I'm not good at playing games!

WOODROW. Sure you are! Don't underestimate yourself. You're great at it!

HELEN. Have you been drinking?

WOODROW. I've had a drink.

HELEN. Well, your reaction to liquor isn't consistent. This time it hasn't made you pleasanter!

WOODROW. That's a popular misconception about liquor. Liquor only heightens the mood you're already in.

HELEN. I'm not in the mood for idle conversation! Will you please leave?

WOODROW. I didn't come for idle conversation.
HELEN. What did you come for?
WOODROW. I came because it's a principle of mine to tell a citizen he's going to be reported. (*Helen says nothing. She waits for him to continue.*) And I'm going to report you as a source of possible undeclared income.
HELEN. (*She thinks she understands.*) I see. (*Cold.*) Very well.
WOODROW. My advice to you is to declare your income and pay tax on it.
HELEN. I don't need your advice. My income tax is not due until next April. You have no indication I'm not going to pay it. I'll thank you to leave or I'll have the house dectective show you out!
WOODROW. I also try to be fair to the taxpayer. You can deduct your expenses. This hotel room—and men's pajamas. (*He goes to the closet and throws open the door.*) The Bureau of Internal Revenue is very understanding. It's been established call girls have expenses.
HELEN. Call girls! (*For a moment Helen is uncomprehending, and then it becomes clear. She stands up speechless. She flops back into the chair in frustrated rage.*) You—you— (*She stands up again. Her anger is too great. She sits again. She stands again, her fists clenched.*) You filthy minded— (*She searches for the word.*) —boy scout! (*She sits again, and now sobs into her hands. Woodrow looks at her a long time, puzzled.*)
WOODROW. (*Finally, foolishly, tentatively.*) Aren't you a call girl?
HELEN. Of course I am! Can't you tell!
WOODROW. No you're not.
HELEN. (*Loudly insistent.*) Yes I am!
WOODROW. I don't believe you. (*He looks around, frustrated. Loudly.*) What do you do in this room?
HELEN. None of your business!
WOODROW. (*A shout, demanding.*) What do you do here?
HELEN. (*After a moment, quietly but not without some pride.*) I have my picture taken in bed with husbands who get divorced! I'm a divorce co-respondent!
WOODROW. Oh! (*He thinks about it.*) Why didn't you tell me?
HELEN. Tell *you*! Mister Big Mouth! The keeper of the country's conscience! You'd run to the Bar Association with a list of my lawyers! If you knew who they were!

WOODROW. (*Stiff.*) I am not an informer! I confine myself to my sworn obligation, which is the Revenue Department!
HELEN. To hell with the Revenue Department!
WOODROW. That comes up every once in a while. Stop crying.
HELEN. Don't tell me what to do. (*But she stops. Woodrow sits.*)
WOODROW. (*Recalling.*) You'd be surprised what I came here for. I lost my nerve. I thought that'd cure me of sleeping pills once and for all. I was short of money. I was going to give you Travelers Checks. (*He looks at her again.*) Well, I apologize again. (*She doesn't answer him, composing her face.*) I seem to do a lot of that. (*A moment.*) You know what? There's no reason for you not to take that job in Paris now. (*Helen turns on him slowly.*)
HELEN. (*Through her teeth.*) I wouldn't take that job in Paris with you if it paid ten thousand dollars a week!
WOODROW. Well, it doesn't pay that. I think you can get a hundred though. As soon as we straighten out your security check. That's what made the trouble. My boss put you up for a civil service rating and they checked on you. That's how they found out about the pajamas and jumped to the call girl conclusion.
HELEN. (*Aghast.*) You mean the United States government has me listed as a call girl?
WOODROW. (*Placatingly.*) Just some departments. It's not official.
HELEN. I'm going to sue you! That's what I'm going to do—I'm going to sue—
WOODROW. It'll all be straightened out— (*The door opens and William Muller enters, thirty-five, dark suit, looking like an arm of the law.*)
MULLER. Miss Bagley?
HELEN. Hello, Mister Knudsen. (*She looks to Woodrow, decides to ignore him.*) Take your coat off, please. (*She goes to the closet for a pajama top.*)
MULLER. (*Looking to Woodrow.*) Who's this gentleman?
HELEN. He's leaving, Mister Knudsen. And would you roll your collar down?
MULLER. I don't think so. And my name isn't Knudsen. (*He takes a leather backed badge from his coat pocket and holds it out.*) It's Lieutenant Detective Muller—of the Vice Squad.
HELEN. Vice Squad?

MULLER. That's right. (*To Woodrow.*) What's your business here?
WOODROW. You're making a mistake, Lieutenant.
MULLER. Am I?
WOODROW. Yes, you are. I'm responsible for your being here. I instigated a security check which mistakenly accused her of being a call girl. That's where your information came from. I assure you it'll all be cleared up tomorrow!
HELEN. That's the truth! (*Muller looks from one to the other, slowly.*)
MULLER. The charge against her isn't as a call girl.
WOODROW. It isn't?
MULLER. She's a professional divorce co-respondent. (*He looks to the pajama top in her hands.*)
HELEN. Oh.
WOODROW. (*Dry throat.*) What does that imply, Lieutenant? Is that a serious charge?
MULLER. She'd be better off as a call girl.
WOODROW. Call your lawyer, Helen. (*She starts.*)
MULLER. His name's Barbee. (*She stops.*) Come on, young lady. You can call him from the district attorney's office. (*Helen takes her purse. Woodrow watches her progress with an agonized expression. As she starts toward the door he speaks.*)
WOODROW. Lieutenant, I'd like to talk to you. (*Woodrow goes to the door and locks it.*)
MULLER. What's that for?
WOODROW. (*It doesn't come easy to him.*) I'd like to make you a proposition.
MULLER. I hope you're not going to offer me a bribe.
WOODROW. This girl had no idea of the gravity of what she was doing.
MULLER. Open the door!
WOODROW. This is a decent girl, Lieutenant. You'll ruin her life. You must have a conscience.
MULLER. I've got my job.
WOODROW. (*Pleading.*) You've also got eyes. This is only a foolish kid. You can see that. She made one slip. We can all do that. (*He reaches into his rear pocket and brings out the checks in billfold.*) I've got twelve hundred dollars in Travelers Checks. Give us a break. You only have to say you didn't find her here.

(*For a long moment Muller looks at him.*) You'll never see her or me again in your entire life. I swear it. (*Muller looks from him to Helen. No hint of assent.*)
MULLER. What good are Travelers Checks?
WOODROW. You can cash them! Anybody'll cash them! (*No response. Frantic now that he's this close, to Helen, as he rushes to the desk.*) She can get the cash from the desk! (*He searches futilely for his pen. Muller gives him his. He starts to sign his name on the checks, quickly.*)
HELEN. (*Simply.*) I'll be happy to take that job. For any salary.
WOODROW. (*Still signing.*) I haven't got it to give you. I'm quitting!
HELEN. Quitting?
WOODROW. (*Bitterly.*) You can't have it both ways! (*In sarcasm.*) I'm full of principles! Like a boy scout! (*He has finished signing. He gives her the entire billfold. Helen is sick.*) Get the money!
MULLER. Nothing bigger than twenties, miss. (*She nods and starts. She is at the door when a loud buzzing is heard, from Muller. They look to him. Calmly, Muller pulls up his sleeve and shuts off his alarm wrist watch. Smiles.*) My alarm clock. (*He reaches into his pocket and takes out a pill box. He takes a pill.*) Tells me when to take my pills. (*He starts to the water cooler as Helen stares at him. Muller notices.*) What's the matter? Surprised a detective has an ulcer?
WOODROW. Would you mind hurrying? (*With a great effort at keeping calm, she exits. Woodrow sits again, running his hands over his face.*)
MULLER. (*A moment.*) Think it's going to rain?
WOODROW. I don't know. I didn't notice.
MULLER. We can use some rain.
WOODROW. I guess so.
MULLER. Paper said rain. Hell of a lot they know.
WOODROW. (*Too unhappy to be talkative.*) Well—
MULLER. They make it up. Some guy gets up in the morning and flips a coin. That's the job I'd like. Flip a coin in the morning and you're through for the day— (*The door is flung open. Butch and Joey enter, followed by Gladys and Helen.*)
GLADYS. (*From deep down.*) That's him!
JOEY. (*Recognizing him.*) Yeah!

GLADYS. Now you're a cop! With a badge!
HELEN. (*To Woodrow.*) He's not a detective!
WOODROW. (*Lost.*) He isn't?
GLADYS. He thought he'd shake her down. I told him all about her. In bed. Pillow talk to keep him amused.
MULLER-PATTERSON. I needed a couple of hundred bucks. He offered me the money.
BUTCH. (*Evenly, never having taken his eyes from his prey.*) I'll have to ask everybody to leave this room. Almost everybody.
JOEY. Gladys!
GLADYS. I've got a better idea! Joey, put a pajama on him!
JOEY. Say! Yeah!
GLADYS. We're getting a divorce, Mister Patterson! (*Joey rushes to the closet, takes a discarded top.*)
HELEN. (*Starting to take off her dress.*) My pleasure, Gladys!
GLADYS. Stay out of that bed! (*She starts to take her own dress off.*) I wouldn't let you go that near him! Something might rub off! (*To her husband.*) Take your coat off! (*He doesn't move.*)
BUTCH. (*Quietly.*) The lady says take your coat off! (*Joey helps him take it off, and puts the pajama top on him, fastening it around his neck. He gets in bed. Gladys pulls the sheet in position to conceal her face. Joey takes the camera.*)
GLADYS. Okay, Butch.
BUTCH. (*Never moving. Steely.*) I see you, Mister Patterson, in bed with a woman!
JOEY. (*Cold.*) Watch the birdie! One—two—three! (*Gladys gets out of bed, as does her husband.*)
WOODROW. Is that what you did?
HELEN. Uh huh.
WOODROW. (*To Joey.*) You know, she's really his own wife!
JOEY. Yeah. That's a very interesting legal point.
BUTCH. (*As Muller-Patterson puts his coat on.*) I'll escort you out of the hotel.
GLADYS. Nothing doing, Butch! You got a wife and five kids. I'm not going to support 'em while you're in jail.
BUTCH. I promise I won't lay a hand on him. (*He raises his hand.*) I swear on my kids. (*He holds the door open for Muller-Patterson.*) This way. (*They start out.*)
GLADYS. Go with 'em, Joey! So he doesn't forget! (*Joey does.*)
HELEN. (*Handing the billfold to Woodrow.*) Here's your money.

GLADYS. What did you give it to him for?
WOODROW. He was going to arrest her.
GLADYS. She'd've gotten a suspended sentence.
WOODROW. I don't think so. If he'd been a real detective.
GLADYS. Judges get divorced too. There've been two in that bed.
HELEN. (*To Woodrow.*) Can I have that job now? (*Tentatively.*) Or any other job you care to—offer me.
WOODROW. (*Looking at her.*) I guess so. I can't keep taking sleeping pills. We can be married on the boat if we can get a license in time.
HELEN. I know a man at the license bureau. We won't have to wait. Just slip him a few dollars— (*Woodrow eyes her. Hastily.*) We'll wait! (*Butch and Joey enter. Butch crosses to the telephone, all watching him.*)
BUTCH. (*Into phone.*) Molly, Butch! Call an ambulance! Somebody fell down a whole flight of stairs! (*To Gladys.*) I never laid a hand on him.
JOEY. That's right. He tripped over his foot.
BUTCH. (*Into phone.*) He's lying on the bottom of the fourteenth floor. (*He hangs up.*)
GLADYS. You mean the fifteenth floor.
BUTCH. No, the fourteenth floor. As soon as he comes to he's going to fall down another flight of stairs. (*MacKelwaine enters. He is an embittered man.*)
HELEN. Why, Mister MacKelwaine! I thought you were on your honeymoon!
MACKELWAINE. Well, you're wrong! I'm on my divorce! (*Starting to take his coat off.*) I want my picture taken.
HELEN. (*Flustered.*) We're expecting someone who has an appointment—
MACKELWAINE. You're expecting me! It's my appointment! I'm Knudsen! And don't tell your old boss I was here! I don't need his horse laugh!
HELEN. The place is under new management, or really, old management. This is the original Miss Bagley.
GLADYS. How do you do.
MACKELWAINE. How do you do.
GLADYS. Help him, Joey.
MACKELWAINE. Never mind, I know the way! (*He goes toward*

the pajama closet and takes a pair.) I'm going to get a pair of pajamas with my initials on! (*He starts to put the coat on.*)
HELEN. Goodbye, Gladys. I'll write you from Paris.
GLADYS. Do that.
WOODROW. Goodbye.
GLADYS. Take care of each other. (*She shakes hands with Woodrow.*)
WOODROW. (*Reluctant.*) I'm sorry, but I have to tell you I'm going to report you as possible unreported income. (*Helen is shocked. She shrugs to Gladys.*)
GLADYS. (*She smiles at Woodrow.*) Okay, sonny. I'll pay my income tax.
WOODROW. (*Pleased.*) If you ever get to Paris come and see us.
GLADYS. I might.
HELEN. (*At the door.*) Au revoir!
WOODROW. Au revoir!
ALL. Au revoir! (*They exit.*)
GLADYS. (*To Butch and Joey.*) Go on, boys! (*They leave. MacKelwaine gets in bed, Gladys is undressing.*) You've been in this bed before?
MACKELWAINE. (*He nods.*) Uh huh. Do I get a reduced rate?
GLADYS. (*Smiles.*) Not a dime.
MACKELWAINE. (*He looks at her.*) You want to have a drink with me some place?
GLADYS. (*Conscious of her appearance, her hand to her face, both for the nose and to cover her eye. MacKelwaine gently takes her hand down.*) Are you crazy?
MACKELWAINE. (*Softly.*) We could go someplace dark. (*Touching.*) I'm lonely!
GLADYS. (*Same tone.*) Who isn't? (*She looks at him a moment, agreeing. Joey and Butch enter.*)
BUTCH. I see you, Mister MacKelwaine, in bed with a woman!
JOEY. Watch the birdie! One—two—three. (*The curtain comes down on the tableau, as a still picture.*)

PROPERTY PLOT

ACT ONE

SCENE 1 (Office)

On Stage:

- Leather couch
- Desk, with:
  - Pad and pencil
  - Notary Seal
  - 2 telephones
  - Typewriter
- Purse, in desk
- File cabinet
- Wastebasket

Off Stage:

- Pipe (Barbee)
- Hand towel, Compact etc., Whiskey and soda (Helen)
- Small parcel (containing pajamas) (MacKelwaine)

SCENE 2 (Elevator)

On Stage:

- Elevator intercom
- Wrist watch (Helen)

SCENE 3 (Restaurant booth)

On Stage:

- Restaurant booth (or table and 2 chairs)
- Place settings, for dinner (2)
- Small package (containing perfume) (Woodrow)

Off Stage:

- Menus (2), Tray with 2 bowls of soup, Pad and pencil (Waiter)

Scene 4 (Hotel room)

On Stage:

Dressing table, with mirror
Telephone
Desk
Assorted chairs
Typewriter
Murphy bed (foldaway) with sheets, blankets, pillows
Camera, with flash (Joey)
Derby hat (Butch)
Deck of cards
Newspaper, Money clip, with bills, Property settlement (3 copies) (Barbee)
Wrist watch (MacKelwaine)
Pajama tops, on hangers in closet

Off Stage:

Purse, containing Notary Seal, pen and compact (Helen)
Alarm wrist watch, Purse, containing appointment book (Gladys)
Wallet, with four $50 bills (Mr. Brown)

Scene 5 (Office)

On Stage:

Perfume bottle, in desk drawer
Purse, with appointment book, on desk

Off Stage:

Letter (Barbee)

Act Two

Scene 1 (Hotel room)

On Stage:

Small phonograph, with records (including "Teach Yourself French" record)
Stand, for phonograph
Bowls of flowers
Assorted books and magazines (one book open by chair, for Butch)
Large European travel poster, on wall

Deck of cards
Pad and pencil
Camera } (Joey)
Mexican postcard } (Joey)
Neat stacks of pajama tops, in closet (cellophane-wrapped)
Black dress, for Helen, in closet
Hangers, in closet

Off Stage:
Hat box and assorted packages (Helen)
Purse, with handkerchief (Gladys)
Wallet, with bills (Turner)

SCENE 2 (Restaurant booth)

On Stage:
Wallet, with photo of mother (Woodrow)

Off Stage:
Menus (2) } (Waiter)
Tray with 2 bowls of soup } (Waiter)
Pad and pencil } (Waiter)
Handkerchief (Turner)

SCENE 3 (Police station)

On Stage:
Wooden bench
Raised desk, with:
  Telephone
  Pad and pencil
Wet handkerchief (Turner)

Off Stage:
Business card (Haskell)
Pad, with paper and pen (Policeman)

SCENE 4 (Hotel room)

On Stage:
Camera, with flash } (Joey)
Basin of water } (Joey)
Towel } (Butch)
Small bottle of coagulant } (Butch)
Small mirror } (Gladys)
Wrist watch } (Gladys)
Water cooler

Off Stage:

Purse } (Helen)
Wrist watch }

Police badge, in pocket }
Alarm wrist watch } (Muller)
Pillbox, with pill }

Traveler's checks (Woodrow)

- ☐ YOU KNOW I CAN'T HEAR YOU WHEN THE WATER'S RUNNING
- ☐ WE HAVE ALWAYS LIVED IN THE CASTLE
- ☐ AMERICA HURRAH
- ☐ HOME FREE
- ☐ COME SLOWLY, EDEN
- ☐ LITTLE BROTHER: LITTLE SISTER
- ☐ SOMETHING I'LL TELL YOU TUESDAY
- ☐ FRAGMENT OF A LAST JUDGMENT
- ☐ WIDOW'S MITE
- ☐ THE LILIES OF THE FIELD

DRAMATISTS PLAY SERVICE, Inc.

440 Park Avenue South, New York, N. Y. 10016